Zora Neale Hurston

African-American Literary Investigations

Ronald Jacobs
General Editor

Vol. 1

PETER LANG
New York • Washington, D.C./Baltimore • Boston • Bern
Frankfurt am Main • Berlin • Brussels • Vienna • Canterbury

Ayana I. Karanja

Zora Neale Hurston

The Breath of Her Voice

PETER LANG
New York • Washington, D.C./Baltimore • Boston • Bern
Frankfurt am Main • Berlin • Brussels • Vienna • Canterbury

Library of Congress Cataloging-in-Publication Data

Karanja, Ayana I.
Zora Neale Hurston: the breath of her voice / Ayana I. Karanja.
p. cm. — (African-American literary investigations; vol. 1)
Includes bibliographical references.
1. Hurston, Zora Neale—Criticism and interpretation.
2. Literature and anthropology—United States—History—20th century.
3. Women and literature—United States—History—20th century. 4. Afro-Americans
in literature. 5. Afro-Americans—Folklore. 6. Folklore in literature. I. Title. II. Series.
PS3515.U789Z76   813'.52—dc20   95-22322
ISBN 0-8204-2857-4
ISSN 1081-9460

Die Deutsche Bibliothek-CIP-Einheitsaufnahme

Karanja, Ayana I.:
Zora Neale Hurston: the breath of her voice / Ayana I. Karanja.
–New York; Washington, D.C./Baltimore; Boston; Bern;
Frankfurt am Main; Berlin; Brussels; Vienna; Canterbury: Lang.
(African-American literary investigations; Vol. 1)
ISBN 0-8204-2857-4
NE: GT

Cover art by Arlene Turner Crawford
Cover design by Lisa Dillon

The paper in this book meets the guidelines for permanence and durability
of the Committee on Production Guidelines for Book Longevity
of the Council of Library Resources.

© 1999 Peter Lang Publishing, Inc., New York

Printed in the United States of America

Dedication

This work is a tribute to the loving memory of my parents,
Virginia Lowe Bassett and Arthur Wesley Bassett

Affirmations

I remember the early visionaries . . .
Bettye Jean (Mbitha) Smith, Lillian Anthony, Rita Arditti, Iva
      Carruthers,
            Jean Thomas Griffin, Hortense Spillers, and Gloria
            Smith.

Deep gratitude to my beloved students, some of whom are:
      Angie Whitmal, Tara Betts, Natalie Howse, Justin Evans, Heather
          McMillan, Tatia Miller, Will Bowens, Majorie
             Michel, Cindy Fullilove, Jamila C. Williams, Megan
             Ward

The bloodline, the kindred: Barbara, Kitten . . . Lynn, Eric

My children, Cynthia, Jennifer, Donna, Carla, Shakir, Sheria
      & Nia (faith)
      Jamila and Malika

The Priestess: Safiya Karimah; Ulestine—enfolds me in bells 2 divine rhythm.

Sisters of the Yam: Judy Dozier, Arlene Crawford, Sylvia
      Jo Oglesby, Adria, Melbelenia, Barbara Brown (transitioned). Warm
      colleagues—always there—Cheryl Johnson Odim, Susan
      Cavallo Veeder, Pamela Caughie, Diane Suter, Femi Taiwo, Judy
      Wittner.

My husband
         Sokoni
            loved
               me. . . .

Contents

A Note of Gratitude

Dr. Cheryl A. Wall is due a special note of gratitude for the elegantly executed and beneficial compilation of the two-volume work, *Hurston*. These volumes bring together the corpus of Zora Neale Hurston's novels, stories, essays, and folklore collections in a manner most useful to scholars. Quotations and references to Hurston's published works incorporated in *Zora Neale Hurston: The Breath of Her Voice* refer to Dr. Wall's *Hurston*, unless otherwise noted. Any and all errors or inaccuracies contained in *Zora Neale Hurston: The Breath of Her Voice* are mine.

Prologue

(A Woman's Voice): I am the silence that you cannot understand. *I am the utterance of my name.* . . . (Julie Dash, *The Making of an African American Woman's Film: Daughters of the Dust,* 76) [My emphasis]

(Nana Peazant, the matriarch in *Daughters*): We carry these *memories* inside of we. Do you believe that hundreds and hundreds of Africans brought here on this other side would forget everything they once knew? . . . We don't know where the recollections come from. Sometimes *we dream them.* But we carry these *memories* inside of us. . . . Call on those old Africans. . . . They'll hug you up quick and soft like the warm sweet wind. . . . (96). [My emphasis]

Zora Neale Hurston was a major cultivator of an early literary landscape that captured within it a Black woman's consecrated space. The written legacy left by Hurston is a voluminous compilation of expressive productions including ethnography, folklore, novels, and plays, nearly all completed between the early 1920s and 1940s.[1] Viewed retrospectively, Hurston's literary achievements spiraled upward and outward traversing disciplines and genres as she sketched blueprints for new reflective and reflexive approaches to ethnographic writing and recording folklore. With unique literary virtuosity Hurston creatively engaged in textual self-referentiality and unflinchingly wrote herself into the volumes of folklore she collected in Haiti, Jamaica, and islands in the Bahamas. Hurston's writing anticipated postmodernist theorizing about ethnographic practices and prefigured a politics of language and interpretation that would emerge on a grander scale in the discipline in the late 1970s. The folklore and ethnographic writing into which she artfully inserted her voice, thoughts, and feelings foretold shifts in the conceptualization of research methods and ethnographic writing that would challenge prevailing paradigms and discourses in anthropology some fifty years after publication of most of her ethnographic fiction and two major collections of folklore.[2]

Hurston pushed the boundaries of ethnographic writing in a fashion similar to ethnographers who are now referred to as postmodernist[3] anthropologists—those who challenge conventional forms of ethnographic writing and who demonstrate unconventional discursive practices. These new discourses aim to dissolve barriers to appreciating disparate cultural metaphors and symbols. These unconventional ethnographic discourses also raise questions about the legitimacy of master narratives and literal textual meanings. In other words, relying on inductive reasoning postmodernist ethnographers heed neither symbols nor signs as fixed and immutable within a cultural context. Their brand of ethnography subverts conventional ways of positing notions of the 'real world' and in an important sense treats the claims of such methods with deep skepticism. Postmodernist anthropologists' view of ethnographic writing stands in contradistinction to the hegemonic agency they believe to be present in much of the ethnography produced during the "modernist period"[4] in anthropology. Thus postmodernism might be perceived as a reaction against the staid attempt at realism which attended the ethnographic writing of the modernist period. Theorist Fredric Jameson draws a distinction between "modernism" and "postmodernism," viewing the former as "scandalous and offensive to the middle class public—ugly, dissonant, sexually shocking". . . .[5] Commenting on Jameson and *postmodernism* as the term relates to ethnographic writing anthropologist Paul Rabinow notes,

> Although Jameson is writing about historical consciousness, the same trend is present in ethnographic writing: interpretive anthropologists work with the problem of representations of others' representations . . . with the classification, canonization, and "making available" of representations of representations of representations. The historical flattening found in the pastiche of nostalgia films reappears in the meta-ethnographic flattening that makes all the world's cultures practitioners of textuality. . . . Referents are other images, another text, and the unity of the poem is not in the text at all but outside it in the bound unity of an absent book. (*Writing Culture* 250)

Robert Aunger engages the term "textualists" in his essay, "On Ethnography: Storytelling or Science," (*Current Anthropology* 1995: 97) in connection with the notion of the 'book as text,' or a work 'bound up in language,' to describe a school of critical thought related to products associated with postmodern anthropology. Aunger writes,

[A] school critical of traditional ethnography has begun looking at ethnographies as texts to determine how these documents create an "objective" representation of other lifeways in the minds of readers (for examples, see Fabian 1983, Manganaro 1990, Marcus and Fischer 1986, Sanjek 1990, van Maanen 1988). I will call these critics "textualists" because most of them draw their inspiration from the hermeneutic tradition of textual criticism in the humanities. . . . Because it is difficult to know whether ethnographic statements are based on anything more than personal impressions, many ethnographies are convincing only to the degree that the ethnographer has mastered rhetoric. (97)

Indeed, postmodern ethnography departs from 'traditional' or 'conventional' methods in that its proponents and practitioners eschew the use of scientific formulas and deductive reasoning to explain human behavior within culture. Among theorists, or "textualists," as Aunger might call ethnographers whose discourses have gained notice as representative of the postmodern moment in anthropology are Clifford Geertz, Stephen A. Tyler, George E. Marcus, and Michael Fischer. In Geertz's seminal work, *The Interpretation of Cultures* (1973), the stage is set for anthropological theorists and ethnographers to seriously discuss the relative advantages, disadvantages, and deeper meaning for the discipline of reconceptualizing anthropological writing—ethnography in particular—as an imaginative literary enterprise. Declaring that ethnographies *are* fictions Geertz asserts,

Nothing is more necessary to comprehending what anthropological interpretation is, and the degree to which it *is* interpretation, than an exact understanding of what it means—and what it does not mean—to say that our formulations of other peoples' symbol systems must be actor-oriented. . . . In short, anthropological writings are themselves interpretations, and second and third order ones to boot. . . . They are, thus, fictions, fictions, in the sense that they are "something made," "something fashioned". . . . (15)

Clifford's co-edited collection, *Writing Culture: The Poetics and Politics of Ethnography* (1986) is a particularly salient text for my purposes here. *Writing Culture* is a compilation of papers presented by a group of established ethnographers who attended a weeklong interdisciplinary seminar at the School of American Research in Santa Fe, New Mexico, in 1984. Presentations focused on issues related to "the making of ethnographic texts" (vii). Ten scholars attended the meeting, eight of whom are anthropologists, including Paul Rabinow, Vincent Crapanzano, Renato Rosaldo, Mary Louise Pratt, Stephen A.

Tyler, George E. Marcus, and Michael Fischer. Papers from the seminar proceedings are especially significant here, for "All [participants]
were involved in advanced, ongoing work in textual criticism and cultural theory" (*Writing Culture* vii).

Tyler's contribution to the text, *Writing Culture,* titled "Post-
Modern Ethnography: From Document of the Occult to Occult Document" is important because of Tyler's background in linguistic anthropology and the emphasis he places on the poetics of ethnography, or
closing the void between actual speech and writing—an art in which
Zora Neale Hurston was particularly gifted. Tyler compares postmodern
ethnography to the original milieu and intent of poetry and ritual performance suggesting that,

> A post-modern ethnography is . . . in a word, poetry—not in its textual form,
> but in its return to the original context and function of poetry, which, by
> means of its performative break with everyday speech, evokes memories of
> the *ethos* of the community. . . . Post-modern ethnography attempts to rec-
> reate textually this spiral of poetic and ritual performance. (126)

Among the seminar papers Tyler's comments come closest to framing
the intent and content of *The Breath of Her Voice.* Yet I would contend that the postmodern text in its formative stage might well present
itself to the ethnographer devoid of performative *intent* while simultaneously laying the ground for theatrical performance and similar
interpretive reading, as is often the case for Hurston's writing—particularly her folklore collections *Mules and Men* (1935) and *Tell My
Horse* (1938).

In George Marcus's "Contemporary Problems of Ethnography in
the Modern World System" (*Writing Culture*) he notes, "ethnographers of an interpretive bent—more interested in problems of cultural
meaning than in social action—have not generally represented the ways
in which closely observed cultural worlds are embedded in larger, more
impersonal systems" (165–66). Indeed, Marcus's intrigue with political economies embedded within cultural systems when applied to
Hurston's literary and folkloric representations of Black rural southern life raises fascinating questions about the ways in which a town
like that of her youth, Eatonville, Florida—an all-Black town—might
have sustained itself economically. Apart from men such as Hurston's
father who was both a minister and mayor, how might others have
met the economic challenges they surely faced in that region prior to
the turn of the twentieth century? And in what ways might the town's

political economy have influenced the evolution of certain cultural forms that readers have come to know through Hurston's ethnographic and folkloric representations? Afterall, Eatonville was a town at the edge of which there was an imaginary line drawn separating it from the all-White 'other side,' known as Maitland.

Michael Fischer's essay, "Ethnicity and the Post-Modern Arts of Memory," (*Writing Culture*) also from the Sante Fe seminar, suggests that "the modalities of veracity in our age can no longer (if they ever could) be limited to the conventions of realism" (198). It is because of the emergence of notions about writing ethnography in a particular fashion—*now* termed "postmodern"—and advanced by some securely positioned ethnographers that *The Breath of Her Voice*, first written a decade and a half ago, might find an audience. Fischer also points to Walter Benjamin and Sigmund Freud both of whom suggested that, "language itself contains sedimented layers of emotionally resonant metaphors, knowledge, and associations, which when paid attention to can be experienced as discoveries and revelations" (198). Interestingly, the cultural critic and literary theorist, Karla F. C. Holloway has noted the troubled relationship that exists between Black women writers and the English language precisely because of the ways in which language carries and becomes an emotional historical vessel. One reason why Black women writers revise their language, Holloway says, is because

> In colonized Africa, children have been whipped and beaten for using tribal languages in colonial school. For black people on both continents, the English language has a context of abuse and dehumanization. . . . My point is that when black women writers imaginatively engage this English language in their texts, the sociocultural history in these words requires the processes of revision. (*Metaphors* 27)

Thus, postmodernist views notwithstanding, it is imperative that the Black woman "revise" (27) her use of English to accommodate the historical realities of Africans in America and in the African Diaspora. Hurston engaged in a revision of the English language and many Black women writers have followed her example. In the conceptualization and presentation of *The Breath of Her Voice* I too adhere to the cultural and gendered revisionist roadsigns that Hurston erected and modeled decades ago and apply them to the articulation of my ethnographic research and writing. Hurston anticipated and pre-dated the postmodern era in anthropology and her writing, more than that of any other Black literary foremother, profoundly affects Black women's writing today. Indeed, *The Breath of Her Voice* is shaped by a Hurstonian stylistic imprint, for no flat, flaccid presentation could aptly represent the peripatetic spirit of a woman such as she. Zora Hurston's writing continues to encourage women away from the domain of the mainstream to imagine more fitting models for their literary and ethnographic products.

One of the ways in which Hurston demonstated alternative ways of writing is that she often collapsed the boundaries between fact and fiction, as I do in this work. Moreover, I take seriously the view expressed by the sociologist Oyeronke Oyewumi, who in her study, *The Invention of Women: Making an African Sense of Western Gender Discourses* writes,

> Ultimately, in research endeavors, I argue for a cultural, context-dependent interpretation of social reality. The context includes the *social identity of the researcher*, the spatial and temporal location of the research, and the debates in the academic literature. . . . The connections between social identity, *personal experiences*, and the nature of one's research and perspective are complex. Often linkages are unpredictable and nonlinear. (xvi my emphasis)

The *cultural* and *contextual* situatedness of *The Breath of Her Voice* reflect a Black woman's *interpretation* of *social reality* in the sense that my reading of the way in which the 'real world' is constituted, in terms of personal and cultural experience, is likely to be at variance with the interpretation of these notions by Euro-American males, such as those quoted above, notwithstanding certain points of convergence in our theorizing about the nature of postmodern ethnography. These men's *cultural context* and perceptions of *social reality* are likely to be significantly different from mine, for example, in the ways that they might treat the life and work of one of their heroes from the annals of anthropological discourse, in contrast to my treatment of Hurston in this work. Clearly, as Oyewumi suggests, *social identity* and *personal experience* as cultural markers distance them from me. My *research perspective* and writing may well be considered *unpredictable*, especially from the vantage point of the Euro-American male ethnographer despite the relatively recent widespread application of postmodernist thought to writing culture. The dissimilar nature of our culture and power relations and the disjunctive nature of our subject/object social and political locations within culture and society create this substantive perspectival divide.

Contrarily, many examples exist to evidence contemporary Black women writers who make use of non-linear approaches and alternative espistemologies in their works, some of which run parallel to the approach I engage in *The Breath of Her Voice*. In the film *Daughters of the Dust*, for instance, Julie Dash infuses the elder, Nana Peazant, with an unusual sense of time and place as noted in the above epigraph. Further, an examination of Black women's literary breaks with the traditions of mainstream literary styles and other epistemological issues would show—in addition to Dash's film and Hurston's novel, *Their Eyes Were Watching God* (1937), and her collections of folklore—Alice Walker's *The Color Purple* (1982); Gloria Naylor's *Mama Day* (1988); and, Pulitzer Prize winning author, Toni Morrison's *Beloved* (1987), to name but a few notable examples. In each of these works we are given a Black female character who accesses epistemologies that depart from mainstream 'ways of knowing' and codifying reality—modes that fall outside the expected verbal and visual parameters of Western philosophy, systems of thought, and beliefs about the relationship between cause and effect.

An efficacious example of a Black woman's departure from Western thought—a way of perceiving more synchronous with West African belief systems—appears in Gloria Naylor's novel, *Mama Day*. Writing about Naylor's heroine, Miranda, Patricia Hopkins Lattin notes in her essay, "Naylor's Engaged and Empowered Narratee" that,

> the body of the novel *Mama Day* appears to model for the narratee. . . texts that ignore verbal communication. . . . When she actually listens to a voice, Miranda discounts it: A woman points out that all the stories about aliens . . . have told of friendly visitations. . . . Miranda notices a twitch around her mouth and understands that the woman really wants to know how she can sleep at night when she has a husband (a "stranger") who beats her. . . . (CLA 460)

Perhaps more important, placed alongside *The Breath of Her Voice*, Naylor's Miranda upholds the efficacy of dreams as a credible epistemological apparatus within a particular cultural context, for when Miranda wishes to know more about one of her progenitors, Sapphira Wade, Miranda

> searches an old ledger to find something about her ancestor. . . . Miranda finds only a few words on a water-damaged piece of paper that means nothing to her; instead, after an evening agonizing unsuccessfully over *words* she falls asleep and *meets Sapphira in her dreams*. (461 my emphasis)[6]

Part I of *The Breath of Her Voice* is an outcome of archival research and fieldwork and consists of a representation of fieldwork experiences subsumed under the title, "A Sentimental Journey." This segment also contains three pieces of poetic verse inspired by the totality of the Hurston project: "Contemplation," "Nyazema: A Song of Reverie," and "Unforgetfulness." Part I reflects events that both *preceded* and *influenced* the content and context of the dialogue that is the essence of Part II of *The Breath of Her Voice.*

Central to appreciating Zora Neale Hurston's genius, versatility, and identity politics is knowing the ways in which she frequently stepped over disciplinary boundaries in her practice of anthropology, intermixing social science with the humanities so many years in advance of what we now call postmodernist practices within anthropology. Comparable to Hurston's work, interdisciplinarity is a major component of how *The Breath of Her Voice* was conceptualized and is presented. I situate this work at a crossroad—at the place where a tradition of Black women's writing intersects contemporary discursive trends in interpretive, humanistic anthropology.

Part II of *The Breath of Her Voice* consists of four sets of two-part dialogues, teased out of a real-life *dream*, one which I curate much in the manner one might construct a novel around a life event. That is to say, I extracted the essential elements of a dreamscape related to this project and decoded its language. The dream experience was an important historicizing moment in the life of this project and led to the conceptual premise for its presentational format. As a critical impetus to the framework for my writing the dream also places *The Breath of Her Voice* squarely within the tradition of Black women as cultural *writers, scribes,* and *viziers.*

Imagine the voice of the old woman who speaks in Part II of *The Breath of Her Voice* to be one of "those old Africans" (Dash 96) who sometimes appear in dreams, for at the center of my dream was just such an encounter with an old woman, one whose eyes were filled with wisdom and power. The dream made amazingly clear her uncanny acuity at traversing celestial and terrestrial realms, moving between the world of living beings and the space of the spirits of the dead. Paradoxically the image of the old African woman of my dream seemed to be an image interchangeable with Hurston's novelistic Nanny in *Their Eyes.* I pondered whether she simply represented Hurston's fiction or was, perhaps, the legendary heroic magician, Nanny, so often mentioned in Jamaican maroon history. The latter figure is referred to alternately as the "Old Hag," or "Old Hagar." In the language of my dream imaginary, I communicated with the old woman and attempted to reveal my thoughts about the Hurston project. Ignoring these attempts, she only lowered her wrinkled eyelids, set her head perpendicular to the night sky and intoned *sounds* that were literally unintelligible to me, yet their meaning was clear. Thus because of the nature of the old woman's interlocutory role, I forego the insertion of nearly all textual citations.

The first piece of poetic verse, "Contemplation," is an expression of the long period of meditation on the life and work of Zora Neale Hurston this work required. The second piece, "Nyazema: A Song of Reverie," symbolizes the dream of the old woman and the salience of *naming* in traditional African cultures. The third composition, "Unforgetfulness," codifies and connects the dream experience with Part II of the work—the core of the project in which my inquiry around certain events and issues in Hurston's life are mediated by the female ancestral voice. In "Unforgetfulness" I elucidate the old woman's phenomenological form and role as interlocutor, bringing the work full circle.

No doubt in her lifetime some viewed Hurston as trickster-like because of her exuberant personality and unconventional ethnographic practices such as writing herself into two important folklore collections (*Mules and Men* and *Tell My Horse*). By writing in that manner Hurston resisted not only the literary conventions of the mainstream but she also set aside proclamations made by the Black literary vanguard of her day. That is to say Hurston often ignored the dictates of those who constituted the leadership coterie within the New Negro Movement in Harlem during the 1920s and 1930s.

While Euro-American female anthropologists contemporaneous with Hurston, such as Elsie Clews Parsons, Ruth Underhill, Margaret Mead, and Ruth Benedict produced volumes of ethnography that were humanistic in tone, none infused her writing with the type of originality that Hurston consistently demonstrated. For example, Ruth Benedict was an accomplished poet, yet her ethnographic writing did not reveal the poetic sensibility that was so much a part of her identity.[7]

Hurston's contemporary popularity as a novelist, folklorist, and ethnographer notwithstanding, it is among Black anthropologists rather exclusively that she is viewed in her rightful place as a "foremother" in the discipline. And although Hurston has become the subject of important studies in Black literature (Howard 1980; Holloway 1992; Lowe 1995), she may still have come to anthropology before her time.

Notes

1. Although Hurston continued to write beyond the 1940s, her most widely read works were written within this time period.

2. While Hurston remains the most prolific anthropologist who departed from the conventions and the protocols of ethnographic writing in her time, other anthropologists later displayed similar inclinations. See for example, Raymond Firth, *We, the Tikopia*. London: Allen and Unwin, 1936; and Elenore Bowen [Pseud. of Laura Bohannan], *Return to Laughter*. New York: Harper and Row, 1954.

3. The style of ethnographic writing and recording of folklore that Hurston practiced was yet to be named. Today it is called 'postmodern' ethnography.

4. The "modernist period" in anthropology is chronologically disharmonious with that attributed to modernist literature—the latter being typically characterized as the years between the turn of the twentieth century and 1945. In anthropology the "modernist" period—sometimes contested—begins in the 1920s and ends circa 1975. (See Manganaro, "Textual Play, Power, and Cultural Critique: An Orientation to Modernist Anthropology," in Manganaro, *Modernist Anthropology: From Fieldwork to Text*, 3–47).

5. Jameson's discussion of postmodernism appears in his essay, "Postmodernism and Consumer Society," in Hal Foster, *The Anti-Aesthetic: Essays on Postmodern Culture*, 1983.

6. African traditional ways of discernment and knowing (cosmology or meaning-making and epistemology or knowledge and truth) such as are demonstrated in Naylor's work prevail in literature written by Black women throughout the Caribbean, Africa and African Americana.

7. I strongly believe that Ruth Benedict struggled with herself to constrain a poetic voice in ethnographic writing throughout much of her career, only clearly revealing that aspect of herself when writing within the traditional boundaries of the poetic genre.

PART I

A Sentimental Journey

Yale University, James Weldon Johnson Collection

The trip East began on the second day of March 1981. I was filled with exciting and disquieting thoughts. The idea of reaching out in search of traces and poetic accents of Zora Neale Hurston's life was strongly appealing. I left Chicago on a luncheon flight and arrived in New York City to very cold weather. Among my destinations was the Beinecke Library, Yale University. I grappled with thoughts about the easiest way to travel there from where I was staying with friends on the Lower East side. After a few telephone calls, I learned that a train regularly leaves Grand Central Station for New Haven and arrives there in less than two hours. This route seemed the most accessible and direct.

In an earlier telephone conversation with Beinecke Library staff, I requested the forms required of visitors and researchers. Beinecke approved my request for permission to review their Hurston holdings and suggested that two or three days would be sufficient time because of my familiarity with Hurston's work. I wanted to know whether she typed manuscripts or wrote them, on lined or unlined paper, with pen or pencil. Most importantly, I sought clues that might assist me in linking Hurston's life with the deeper meaning of her fictional characters and form.

I scanned original drafts of *Their Eyes Were Watching God; Tell My Horse; Moses, Man of the Mountain,* and *Seraph on the Suwanee.* They catalogue Hurston's manuscripts in first, second, and third draft form. First drafts are neatly written in pencil on unlined, yellow paper. second and third drafts are typewritten. There are few major editorial changes across drafts. She occasionally deletes one or two paragraphs. Observing the seeming ease with which Hurston's writing flows was an embarrassment, for I edit deeply. There was some comfort in knowing that even for one of our most productive and gifted of writers, the craft was evolutionary. Only rarely, I am convinced, does the virgin idea satisfactorily merge with its first written symbols. Every writer's challenge is to "say" what he or she "means." Even though the corpus of Hurston's work is replete with southern folk speech and vernacular language, her first drafts are relatively clean.

My search for remnants of Zora Hurston's life reconnected me with my own past and affirmed meaningful early experiences I had with books and book lovers. Reading always held a primary place in my life. My father enjoyed novels, my mother most often read the newspaper dailies and the *Daily Word*. Through my father, the family subscribed to *National Geographic* over an extended period of years. There were always books in our home. I learned early that books are seductive and inspiring. Their woodsy fragrance, rich beauty, and strong transformative power appeal to something deep within me. As my eyes sweep the printed page, I hear the words' sound and their meaning captivates and lures.

Like me, my two sisters and my brother are consummate readers. We were read to in the evenings, from *Wee Wisdom,* a children's companion piece to my mother's *Daily Word.* In our preteens, we walked to the Hall Branch of the Chicago Public Library carrying shopping bags filled with books to be exchanged for others. This was a Saturday morning ritual. The local library also featured a "story hour" for youngsters. Listening to the "storyteller," we all sat in chairs that later appeared to be appallingly small. The librarian would move her eyes across the pages of books, *speaking* us into other worlds.

I was greatly disappointed that Yale did not allow me to read Hurston and Hughes's controversial play, *Mule Bone.* That the play had been written about elsewhere was an indication of its access to other researchers.[1] My reading of correspondence available at Yale related to the authorship of the play suggests Carl Van Vechten's involvement in the controversy. Van Vechten, a White, male writer, social trend-setter, and confidante of certain Black writers of the Harlem Renaissance, fanned the fire between Hurston and Hughes. Letters written by Hughes to Van Vechten in which Hughes discusses the play, are replete with fretful complaints and accusations against Hurston. The letters also infer that Hurston mysteriously disappeared for several weeks at the apex of the turmoil. For me the correspondence between Hughes and Van Vechten has the connotative effect of "Zora-bash-

Bontemps further expresses his opinion that Hurston is remorseful about problems that she and Hughes experienced in connection with the play.

> [I]f I had a bigger sheet of paper, I could give a lot of reasons why it would be grand if you would recognize [Hurston's] flag of truce. . . . [S]he's never been so well despite her sins of the past. . . . (40)

The letter, dated November 24, 1939, is resonantly gossipy, patronizing, and patently misogynistic. Most important is the manner in which these men devalue Hurston's craft and, alternately, focus on her *behavior*.

Between 1939 and 1953, Hughes's acrimony and sarcasm toward Hurston appears somewhat diminished. A letter written to Bontemps by Hughes approaches the attribution of political savvy to Hurston for the use of Black speech in her writing. Hughes avers Hurston's feeling for Black folk idiom and suggests an authenticity for its place in her work. The following letter excerpt critiques Hurston's literary style and infers some respect for her competence as a writer:

> Dear Arna,
> If you'll tell me what Dick Wright's book is like (since I haven't it) [sic] I'll tell you about James Baldwin's *Go Tell It on the Mountain* . . . . If it [Baldwin's book] were written by Zora Hurston with her feeling for the folk idiom, it would probably be a quite wonderful book. . . . I wish he had collaborated with Zora. (302)

Orlando and Ft. Pierce, Florida

Departing New York was a test of will because an unanticipated snow storm struck the night before my scheduled departure from LaGuardia. The storm crippled the city that night. During the early morning hours of the next day Kennedy and LaGuardia airports were shut down to air traffic. In the late morning I heard that Kennedy might soon re-open. Persisting, then, I stood in high snow drifts, attempting to flag down a taxi driver who would be willing to travel to Kennedy so that I might have a chance to board a flight to Orlando. I located a taxi, arrived at Kennedy, and negotiated a seat on an outbound flight to Orlando—the location from which I would travel to Ft. Pierce. Ft. Pierce is the town in which Zora Hurston spent her last days.

Approaching Orlando from the air, countless large and small water-ways are visible below. The proliferation of lakes is arresting. Upon arrival at the hotel all doubt was removed that the chill plaguing me now for several days had become a full-blown cold. A cold with attendant chills, sore throat, and incessant sneezing. Much to my surprise, Orlando boasted a temperature of 77 degrees; yet I was cold. I searched nearby pharmacies for Vitamin C tablets which typically aid me in the battle against cold miseries. I found none. Oddly my requests raised eyebrows and elicited unexpected responses: "Do you mean the same vitamin that's in orange juice? Oh, no, we haven't anything like that." I resorted to hot tea and Florida sunshine to warm myself—the only person in town wearing a trench coat.

Pressing on to maintain my timetable, I learned that the least costly and, I trusted, the most scenic route to my destination, Ft. Pierce, was by Greyhound bus. In retrospect, a rental car would have been the more practical mode of travel between Florida towns. The bus ride from Orlando to Ft. Pierce takes three hours, and it is not particularly scenic. In March the countryside is not lush and lacks the beauty which I anticipated. The countless lakes and serpentine waterways that appeared beautifully luminescent from the sky became monotonous. Perhaps my compromised health, the New York snow storm, and an interminable bus ride precipitated an alarming sense of doubt about the value of the research in which I was engaged. I knew no one in Ft. Pierce and felt I would probably expend too much time and energy wandering around without meaningful results. Yet my perception of the importance of Hurston's life and work would not permit me to long despair, even though I was uncertain of the fullest extent of my emotions. I only know that misgivings were transformed, replaced by an urgency to see through my research plan; to complete the work I envisioned, no matter the value, or lack of it, that others might attach to it.

But "how would I find Zora's grave?" I recalled that Alice Walker had placed a headstone at the site she identified as Hurston's grave. I reflected on how grateful I was that she had so honored Zora Neale Hurston.[5] I was also reassured of at least one other individual's deep interest in the woman whose life and work fascinated me. "The Garden of the Heavenly Rest," the name of the cemetery in which Hurston is buried, turned over again and again in my mind. Excitement returned, I longed to reach Ft. Pierce.

The Orlando to Ft. Pierce bus ride requires a change in Melbourne, Florida. Confidence rekindled, I wanted as much time in Ft. Pierce as I could carve out. Someone on the bus told me about the possibility of taking a flight from Melbourne to Ft. Pierce on a small aircraft. Pursuing this interest, I found no one who could even confirm the existence of an airport at Melbourne. Frustrated, I began a conversation with a woman who was also riding the bus to Ft. Pierce. This encounter proved to be fortunate. Introducing myself, I then explained my interest in Ft. Pierce and talked about the Hurston research and writing project. The woman at first appeared reluctant to believe that I had traveled to several cities to learn more about a woman whose name she had never heard. She was later convinced of my sincerity and became warm, friendly, and helpful. Annie Lois Milton described herself as an acquaintance of the family who owned one of two "colored" funeral homes in Ft. Pierce: Stones and Peeks. Annie Lois was familiar with both of the older women who used to operate Peeks and with Ms. Peeks's daughter, Sarah, "who is probably taking care of things now," she offered. With obvious pride, my new acquaintance changed the subject and informed me that her son was picking her up at the bus station in Ft. Pierce. "If he doesn't have a car full, I'll be glad to drop you at Peeks," she said, explaining that the funeral home was three blocks from her destination. Although Annie Lois lived in Orlando, it was Ft. Pierce that she most enjoyed because, "it's alive and lively. Orlando is just too dead."

Annie Lois and I talked more about Zora Hurston and Ft. Pierce, about her children and mine. She was shocked by my interest in visiting the cemetery. "Girl," she said, "I don't fool with the dead. Once I picked up my grandbaby from the crib before I realized she was dead and held her for a while. But that was before they took her to the undertaker. When they got through with her, she looked so long, looked like they had stretched her. She looked like she was six years old and was only four months. Honey, I don't mess around with the dead." I concurred with her assessment of the often grotesque, and visually painful outcome of unskilled mortuary science practitioners.

Annie and I talked and laughed easily. She asked whether I might mention her name in the book that I planned to write "I will, if you'd would like me to," I responded. "Oh yes, I do," she assured. I wrote her name and address in the big notebook. She cautioned me to note, "Return to Sender" on my envelope because, "I don't like Orlando and might move back to Ft. Pierce any day now." We boarded the second bus and reached Ft. Pierce an hour or so later. Annie's son, Donovan, was waiting at the depot. They dropped me at the establishment once known as Peeks Funeral home, then called Sarah's Memorial Chapel.

After ringing the bell and rapping on the door several times, I was ready to look elsewhere for someone who could direct me to the Garden of the Heavenly Rest cemetery. Momentarily, I noticed a man crossing the street, walking toward the chapel and motioning in my direction. When he reached the place where I was standing, I introduced myself and asked whether he was associated with the funeral home. He nodded and said, "Yes." Quickly summarizing my research interests, I turned to questions about Zora Neale Hurston. "Oh, come on in," he urged, as he opened the door, gesturing toward a chair. Rufus Smith seated himself behind a small, cluttered desk. "A couple of other people have been down here to look up her grave," he said. Mr. Smith also told me that a sorority had placed a wreath at the site of Zora Hurston's grave a few days before my arrival.

Apparently feeling a need to prepare me for the shock I would soon witness at the cemetery, Mr. Smith mentioned that a woman who recently visited the Hurston grave was obviously disturbed by the cemetery's condition. He explained that his family only recently acquired the property from an old White man who lived up in the Carolinas, that he planned to upgrade the acreage and to make several cosmetic changes. "I had to slash and burn and clear the land myself. Oh, it was a real mess before we got it," he said. Reaching for the telephone, Mr. Smith called a taxi and apologized because he was unable to drive me to the cemetery because all of his cars were in use for funeral services. I inquired whether there was a florist in the area or near the cemetery, explaining my desire to plant flowers at the grave. African Violets and Sedum were my preferences: African Violets would bloom almost constantly and the Sedum is self-propagating. With the Sedum, I envisioned the beauty of nature becoming a green blanket that, in time, would cover Zora Hurston's grave. Mr. Smith commented, "The Flower Patch is a Black-owned business in town." He called The Flower Patch and told them that I would come right over to look for flowers for a grave at the Garden of the Heavenly Rest.

Within ten minutes a taxi arrived with a woman seated next to the driver. As I would later learn, she, too, was a passenger. As I rose from my chair and moved toward the door, it occurred to me that I no longer felt the pull of the camera strap over my left shoulder. Had I left the camera in Annie Lois's son's car, or on the bus? A feeling of disease engulfed me. "Oh, God," I thought, "on the bus!" I thanked Mr. Smith and quickly settled in the taxi, mentally retracing my steps and the conversation with Annie Lois. I recalled the number of the house she gave me in Ft. Pierce. After greeting the taxi driver and passenger and apologizing for taking them off their path, I explained that it was important that I go to the address given to me by Annie Lois. The young man who appeared at the door told me that neither she nor her son had arrived. The next stop was the bus depot. I prayed that our bus was still there. Miracle of miracles, the bus was still in the lot, the door slightly ajar. Worried that it might not be there, I began thinking about the utter importance of this apparatus that we have named "camera"—the way that it stores memories, re-presents past actions and produces images that tell of moments for which there might be no suitable words. The camera was still there, in my empty seat.

The trip from Sarah's Memorial Chapel to the cemetery was actually about five minutes, but we had detoured. For all appearances, Ft. Pierce had few taxis operating and passengers apparently often shared the car. In this instance sharing was an inconvenience to the woman already in the car when I entered at the funeral chapel. The co-passenger, taken out of her way to the bus depot, was obviously quite perturbed. As we reached her destination I said, "I'm sorry for the inconvenience to you." She responded with an inaudible mumble and then said, loudly, "All I wanted to do was go to JCPenney downtown and I've been everywhere but there!" By then JCPenny was but a few yards away and she was delighted to leave us, never replying to my cheerful "Goodbye," except with a fittingly indignant, "Humph!"

The Flower Patch had no Sedum and no African Violets. I chose, instead, several strikingly beautiful Bromeliads for their symbolic value.[6] Interrupting the plant purchase was a man completely hidden behind several rows of hanging, potted plants, and tall philodendrons. He rose now to full height and declared in a loud voice, "I'm Jasper Jones," having overheard my inquiry. "My God, I knew the woman you're talking about. Boy was she something." He was someone with whom I wanted to speak further and asked if I might write to him with questions about Hurston. He agreed to respond and I recorded his name and address in the big notebook.

The ambiance at Ft. Pierce convinced me that the Zora Hurston I knew through her writing would have enjoyed life there. Ft. Pierce called to mind Dakar, Senegal—Ebony faces attached to tall, statuesque bodies outfitted in beautiful bold colors. Sandy-haired children with sun-kissed faces running in every direction. The town was slow-paced and rhythmic; streams of energy flowing and merging from many directions. Brightly painted houses lined the long, narrow, sandy streets. Ft. Pierce was a good place to be that day.

The cemetery was situated at the end of a cul-de-sac. Mr. Smith's half warning about its condition was insufficient preparation for the shock I felt at the sight of the strewn debris that introduced me to Zora Hurston's burial site. The surface of the stone entrance to the Garden of the Heavenly Rest was cracked, fissured, and pitted. The glaring contradiction in all of this lay in the neat and orderly appearance of the handwritten manuscripts Zora had produced, and I read, only days before. Turning into the entrance, the taxi driver said, "This is it." I paid the fare and moved on to the grounds. In the distance smoke spiraled upward from small bundles of smoldering dead grass, weeds, and debris that encircled the cemetery. While at Sarah's, Mr. Smith had given instructions on how to find the grave: "When you come in the gate," he had said, "look off to the right and you'll see a headstone sticking up out of the ground. It's the only one out there. You can't miss it." He was right. Off a short distance inside the stone facade my eyes quickly caught a glimpse of the only headstone in this vast space of sand, weeds, and spiraling soft blue smoke. I approached Zora's grave with hesitation and humility. Despite the obviously neglected cemetery, I was awed in the presence of Zora Hurston's spirit. There was no doubt that the woman buried in this neglected place had had a prolific and profound life as a writer. The irony of her life struck me at that moment in a way that I had not before experienced. "There are two root causes related to this tragedy, this uncanny reality: Zora Neale Hurston was Black and female and both she and the literary products which she generated were grossly devalued." For these reasons she died in a welfare home and was buried in a potter's field. Before Alice Walker placed a marker at her grave, there was nothing there to celebrate her life or commemorate her death. I mused: "Consider the web that connects the masses of Black women's lives, time and place notwithstanding. Are these not the same forces that had intruded upon my consciousness and created doubt and undervaluation of my own work?" Standing at Zora Hurston's grave I felt both anger and pride. Later, contemplating the meaning of that day, I knew that all was well with Zora Neale Hurston and with me. With a lighter heart, I soon traveled to Eatonville, Florida.

The Eatonville Experience

Macedonia Baptist Church was holding Sunday morning service when I arrived in Eatonville. The church had a contemporary facade, obviously having undergone restoration since Zora Hurston's youth. I stopped an old woman just before she entered and asked whether she remembered the Hurston family. She had no recollection of Zora, nor did she know any members of her family. The topic of interest for her was the general condition of Black people in America. Our brief discussion took a turn in that direction, but was foreshortened by the fact of her tardiness to service.

The town seemed curiously quiet that morning, yet I was anxious to identify spaces within its geographic boundaries and landscape which I might associate with Hurston's descriptions of Eatonville. Notebook in hand, I wanted to continue recording events and conversations as I had since the beginning of my journey. The taxi driver who delivered me from Orlando to Eatonville knew little about the town. He responded to my comment about the town's quiet, saying, "Most folks are still asleep after last night's partying; they're not all in church!" I talked about Eatonville's status as an all-Black town. The mention of race drew him out. His observations on the subject were keen and politically astute. He commented on the effects of a racialized society on Blacks with deep insight. Development of a viable economic base was, he believed, the strategy Blacks should embrace.

Walking along a street in Eatonville I noticed a grocery store with a front porch that could easily have been Joe Clarke's. His store front porch was the heart of Hurston's community in *Their Eyes*. It was the platform from which on any given evening "lies," large and small, issued from the mouths of its inhabitants. From her autobiographical work, *Dust Tracks on a Road*, we learn that Joe Clarke's was the place to which she yearned to go on errands. Once there, it was possible to eavesdrop as men verbally recreated and enlarged their worlds. I felt excitement as I came closer to the store and could see human forms seated on benches on the front porch. Approaching the store, a sign became visible in the window. It read: "West-Indian & American Groceries." An old gasoline pump had found its way to the porch, a relic whose displaced appearance added intrigue to the moment. The porch was a concrete slab, about thirty feet in length. Three old men sat on benches under two large windows that were separated by a screened doorway. A second sign, smaller than the first, advertised the *Orlando Sentinel Star*.

The cane on which the first old man leaned appeared to be an unusual walking stick. Upon closer view I realized that the stick was the type African chiefs and diplomats carry on special ceremonial occasions, or are part of their attire when visiting a foreign country. The first elder gentleman wore white trousers, a brown jacket, and a hat like the one worn by my father when I was growing up. The hat had a wide brim, a moderately high crown and a grosgrain band of about two inches in width that separated the crown and brim. His legs crossed, arms folded in his lap as he sat there—still, and poised in the shadow of a wooden awning.

A second old warrior shared the bench with the first. He appeared younger and was dressed in an arresting combination of clothes: a luminous yellow, fiberglass cap; something between a baseball cap and a hard hat. He also wore black and white trousers with a large checkered pattern, a blue print shirt and brown jacket. Sitting sprawl-legged, hands palm down—resting on the bench—he appeared ready to hoist himself up at a moment's notice. Holding that pose, he only swiveled his head from left to right as he observed shoppers come and go.

I approached these two elders with a smile and introduced myself. Succinctly explaining my work, I asked in a voice loud enough for both to hear, "Did either of you ever know a woman by the name of Zora Hurston, or did you know the Hurston family?" The first of the two pondered my words a few moments and replied, "No. I sho didn't." I asked how long he'd lived in Eatonville. "I come here in nineteen 'n nineteen," he responded. (I knew that by 1919 Zora Hurston was a student at Howard University). There was small likelihood that he would have known Zora Hurston. Hearing my question, without a word, the second old one swiveled his head from left to right, lasting just long enough to be sure that I had observed his nonverbal response.

At the opposite side of the porch, I greeted the third elder. Sitting erect, he wore crimson trousers and also tightly clutched a staff in a fist that resembled aged, weather worn, dark brown grainy leather. The impression he gave was of a man who had rendered a profound statement only moments earlier and added emphasis to it with a dramatic raising and down-pounding of his staff. Yet he was a quiet man, with soft, watery eyes that sharpened the color of his trousers, making them more striking. He, too, sat cross-legged, never allowing our eyes to meet. He responded to my question with a slow, warmly quiet, "No." The two-lettered word lingered on the air like the last note of a great symphony.

I asked the old ones whether they would allow me to take their picture. Either verbally, or by facial expression each agreed to sit for a photograph. Without rearranging themselves in any way, the first two looked towards me, and the third looked away as I squeezed the shutter button three separate times. I thanked them for their images and for their contributions to this work. Completing the old ones' photographs, I noticed a younger man leaving the store; a man far younger than the porch-sitters. I approached him and asked the Hurston family "question series" for the sake of continuity, understanding the unlikelihood of him knowing them. When I asked to photograph him, he backed away saying, "I don't think you'd better; could be the CIA or something like that. You never know what's going on these days." I agreed with his assessment of "what's going on" and left him to go on his way.

I then observed a very young man of twelve or thirteen leave a bicycle on the grass in front of the store. Wanting to talk with him, I waited to see him exit the store and retrieve his bike. The nature of my curiosity in this instance was related to knowing whether Hurston's books were in the local schools and whether the youth had an awareness of her as a heroic literary figure. Quite suddenly the young man slammed the screen door against the wall, moved swiftly towards his bike, mounted it, and charged headlong up the street. All hope of an interview dashed.

Across the street was a neat, two-story, square brick building that bore on its facade: "Ethel's Tavern." Curtains hung at the upstairs windows, giving the impression that the building served a dual purpose. Five or six young men stood outside Ethel's. Apparently they had observed the photo-shoot with the old men. "Why don't you take a picture of something that *really* looks good," one shouted, raising his right arm in a "Black Power" kind of way. I accommodated and photographed him and his cheering supporters. They all applauded. The conviviality of the previous night's mood remained operative. A few yards from them was a small, brick-faced building that resembled a large fireplace. Centered immediately above the entrance I read, "Town Hall, Eatonville, Fla. 32751." I thought it odd that the Zip Code was posted on the building with a street address.

I walked towards a sign on a road that ran perpendicular to Eatonville's main artery. The sign read "Clarke Street." I imagined that the street was named in honor of Joe Clarke, the man who envisioned the all-Black town that became known as Eatonville and was incorporated on August 18, 1886. Turning off Clarke Street, I approached another large sign: "Maitland City Limits." The bifurcation of the larger city, Maitland, in 1886, was accomplished to create the all-Black township of Eatonville—clearly a historically significant moment. The ramifications of this action cannot be overestimated for the Black cultural treasure trove that the town became, relatively free from critical gaze, influence, and domination of all-White Maitland.

Zora Neale Hurston's writing reflects a fondness not only for Black culture, but also for nature; aspects of the natural world are important figurations in her fiction. In *Their Eyes*, there is the pear tree imagery of emergent, youthful female sexuality, as well as the hurricane, the omen of death. The spider on the wall foretelling Lucy's death in *Jonah's Gourd Vine* is another such example. The Chinaberry tree in Eatonville about which Hurston often writes ranked high in the inventory of visual landscape images I wished to capture for this project. In search of this specimen, I strolled along a heavily vegetated street where I noticed a man exiting a space between a clump of bushes and small trees. I called out to him, "Sir, could you please tell me which of these trees is a Chinaberry?" He first seemed startled or puzzled, then turning his focus skyward he began spinning round and round. I am certain that he wondered how it was possible that anyone would not recognize a Chinaberry tree when they saw one. After all, I was in a region where they abound. I made no attempt to explain my ignorance. There was a pause in his turning as he pointed in front of himself toward the trunk of a tree slightly hidden in the thicket. Somewhat ruefully he exclaimed, "Why there's one right there!" I moved closer and examined the texture of the trunk and limbs only to discover abject nakedness—no leaves! "Where are all of the leaves?" I complained. Everything else in my view was a lush green. Noting my disbelief and disappointment, he replied, "Oh, uh, Chinaberries don't get their leaves 'til fall." How relieved I was to know that this bareness was impermanent. Were it not so, how would I interpret Hurston's fondness for them? Thanking my aid several times for his patience, I photographed the dormant specimen. In other woodsy spaces in Eatonville I recognized Chinaberry trees again and again. Strong, tall Chinaberries with outstretched limbs curved just right to cradle a day-dreaming, pre-pubescent girl.

I never met anyone in Eatonville who could say much about Zora, or her family, but I found the townspeople charming. Especially striking was the old Black woman I met early on Sunday morning, striding toward the entrance to Macedonia Baptist Church.

Notes

1. Controversy continues over which writer, Hurston or Hughes, deserves credit for the majority authorship of the play, *Mule Bone*. In my view the only clear aspect of the issue is that the play is based on Hurston's short story, "The Bone of Contention."

2. The suggestion here is that Hughes's parodic use of Southern, folk idiomatic speech, such as he frequently used above his signature on letters to Van Vechten, was done in a manner not in keeping with the serious nature of the letters themselves and suggests an attempt to ridicule Hurston's consistent use of the language of the Black rural South. Hughes might, for example, complain about Hurston's behavior in "standard English," yet close his letter with words approximating a statement such as "Yours 'til chicken stops fryin' in grease." Another possible interpretation might be that Hughes wished to acknowledge Van Vechten's place as a White male who believed himself well versed in "Negro" culture.

3. Despite the heightened collective consciousness among Black literary artists, and other creative individuals who found their way to Harlem at the turn of the twentieth century and its first two decades, Arnold Rampersad notes, "underneath this impressive demonstration of talent and optimism . . . a variety of disparate individuals were 'made to conform to [Alain] Locke's perception of a new breed of Negroes in a brave new world of Negroness. Wishing to impress largely white readers with the sophistication of the New Negro, Locke ignored much of popular culture, including the blues. . . . Indeed, deep strains would eventually burden the relationships among Hughes, Cullen, Toomer, and Hurston" (Mullane 479).

4. *Tell My Horse* is a mixed genre—a compilation of Haitian and Jamaican cultural practices observed and recorded during Hurston's fieldwork in those countries. Much of the book's content reflects certain West African traditional religion, commonly referred to in New World literature as Vodoo. The work includes short ethnographies, songs, recipes, stories, photographs, and myths. Among the photographs is one of Hurston poised over a Congo drum as if ready to sound the instrument. *Tell My Horse* was also published in 1939 in England under the title *Voodoo Gods*.

5. I reread Walker's "In Search of Zora Neale Hurston" upon my return home and found deeper resonance with it—no doubt a result of my own experience in Harlem, Eatonville, Ft. Pierce, and other places where I sought a deeper understanding of the environment that shaped Hurston.

6. Bromeliads grow out from great tree trunks in forested areas. In Egyptian mythology, Isis, the great goddess has multiple manifestations, one of which is as the goddess, Hathor, who is called, "Lady of the Sycamore Tree." A Bromeliad, then, might be thought of as a manifestation of the great goddess Isis/Hathor.

Contemplation
(A Lighted Candle)

Ancient mother of the seas,
  your womb, a vessel of sacred blood.
You make mountains with your wings and
    stars fall from your mouth.
    Pierce the night with mystic eyes.
Ride the spray of my breath, the sound of my voice
    to the cusp of yesterday.
Hear the sound of my words playing on the wind.
    Wrap my voice in your hair;
    awaken the daughter/spirit in your bosom-nest.
    Sing the song of her primeval name.
    Ride the breath of my voice.
        Ride the breath of the wind.
    Ride the breath of my voice.
        Ride the breath of the wind.
Hear the breath of her voice on the sound of the wind.
    Voices moving . . . mooooving . . . moooooooving.
Nyazema breathes; her voice sings re/memberings.
    Hear the breath of my voice.
    Hear the breath of my words.
        Feel the spray of her voice.
        Feel the spray of her words.
    Our voices soar on the edge of the wind.

Nyazema: A Song of Reverie

Old Woman of Fallen Breasts Sings:
    Nyazema, Nyazema, Nyazemaaaaaaaaa,
    child/woman, girl, child/woman, woman, girl/woman/child.
    Breathing deeply, the old one wails—hurls her name into
        the wind. Nyazemaaaaaaaaaa-spirit of forever.
    Nyazema, beguiling woman of ancient yesterdays!

The Dreamer: Startling images darting, whirling, spiraling, form and
        vanish
            from the dreamscape of my night eyes.
    I dream worlds of dreams, dream of worlds unseen.
    Oh life, oh life, oh life. Primeval voice, whirl, loooooooooop,
        fuse with this Sister-song I sing. I sing a Sisterful,
            borne
        Black womansong. I sing and sing my song, unreel
            your voice.
    Zooooooooop! I catch the wind in my teeth, hold tight to her
        name, singing a Sisterful, borne Black womansong.
        Sisterful, borne Black womensing songs of life—of suns
            and moons, and timeless rites.
        Spinning, spinning in my reverie of forever-dreams.
        Floating stars kiss my moonlit eyes.
        Magnetic aroras flash, a fire-night constellation
            somersaults, falling over, over, over,
            entangling my hair.
        Fire red alphas zing, flash, dance, flicker in time with
            her name:

Nyazema, Nyazema, Nyazema.
She re/members her name, she re/members her song.
Singing, her song, she heaves up, up, up, heavens of
        light
                words from the deep darkness of her russet
                throat—
Reveries of her thick life (2B) mined.

Unforgetfulness

Dreams dissolve upon my face—melting
sheets of cotton candy floating, adrift on river
      beds of flowers wilted in the heart of yesterday.
Where is the woman in the moon at sunset?
She slivers into small, opaque spaces, between canyon walls
      where time awaits the unknown.
Clapping voices thrown down long corridors turn sharply at the
      boldness of her words—words wet with hand-crafted, mojo
      messages, falling on deafness, shivering resonantly, unprotected
      in the cold, night air.
Memories—lightly rolled parcels lay chaste in a silken corner of your
      mind; hauntingly rounded by time, their angularity rubbed,
      smooth-edged in disguise.
Dreams make music and clamor for life in unfathomed openness,
      infatuated by a chance meeting with their own kind.
Tricksters, whose fanciful masks race forward, raging, then backward,
        fleeing.
Tricksters walk upside down on walls, in water, spin on rainbow rays,
      and misty morning dew. Their wizard-hearts tango through
      hoards of the rudely unaware, fill an akward moment's heavy
      silence, lift images of winged-things, anxious to fly South—
      fly South to paradise.
She remembers a summer's day, its long, long forgotten crispness,
      falling shadows engulfed miles travelled across a salty, flat
      journey. Old, dry, thirsty memories, called to life from nowhere,
      heaped up, confessing the nakedness of time.
Old Hagar turns inside out, divining fields in search of lost dreams,
      etched in languid word-pools. She rolls over hills, fertile with
      indigo, rooted in darkness, scattering dust at daybreak, and chants.

1. Fissured stone wall, Garden of the Heavenly Rest cemetery, Ft. Pierce, Florida, 1981 (Photograph Credit: Ayana I. Karanja)

2. Zora Neale Hurston's grave, Garden of the Heavenly Rest cemetery, 1981. Headstone donated by Alice Walker. (Photograph Credit: Ayana I. Karanja)

3. Town Hall, Eatonville, Florida, 1981. (Photograph Credit: Ayana I. Karanja)

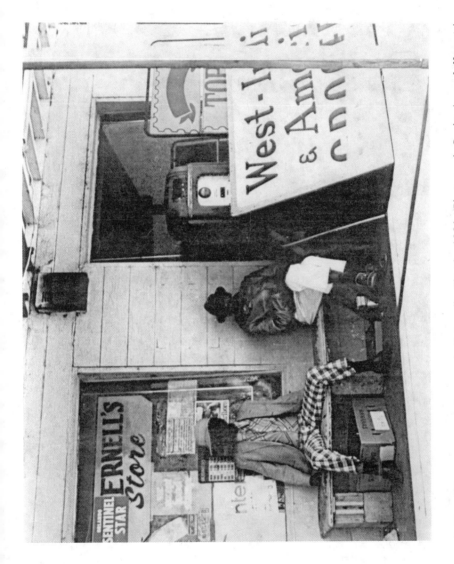

4. Men sitting on grocery store porch, Eatonville, Florida, 1981. (Photograph Credit: Ayana I. Karanja)

5. Youth with a bicycle in front of grocery store, Eatonville, Florida, 1981. (Photograph Credit: Ayana I. Karanja)

PART II

New Moon: The Child Woman

Ships at a distance have every man's wish on board. For some they come in with the tide. For others they sail forever on the horizon, never out of sight, never landing until the Watcher turns his eyes away in resignation, his dreams mocked to death by Time. That is the life of men. Now, women forget all those things they don't want to remember, and remember everything they don't want to forget. The dream is the truth. Then they act and do things accordingly.

Zora Neale Hurston, *Their Eyes Were Watching God*

Frequently one finds difficulty disputing allegations made by others who believe that certain events have occurred and suggesting that what is 'factual' or 'knowable' has been revealed in a a given circumstance. There are readers and critics who have either stated or implied, for example, that there is very little substance to be found in your autobiography, *Dust Tracks on a Road* (1942). They have also suggested that you are dishonest about the information that the book provides. These assessments may be valid or invalid, and I suppose this issue falls under the rubric of subjective value. The general concern seems to be less about "facts" or "accuracy" and more related to the non-confessional nature of *Dust Tracks*. I believe that *Dust Tracks* represents as much as you desired to share with the world at that particular place and time. I mean, simply, that only you could judge what should be revealed and what ought to remain private. You also know that your critics accuse you of "entertaining" relationships with Whites. The inference is that you only revealed as much in *Dust Tracks* as you could without running the risk of damage to your relationships with them.

It seems to me that one ought to have the privilege to reveal as much as one feels is appropriate or desirable and, similarly, to retain personal privacy. The problem has more to do with the fact that "the public" begins to feel a right of ownership to the private lives of public persons. Anything less than full disclosure—or what "the public" perceives as less—is cause for alarm, if not ridicule. Convinced as I am, however, that the inner self of the literary personality, probably more than any other public, or quasi-public person, is evidenced in the products of their craft, I have sought to know the "true" Zora Neale Hurston through your writing. I decided to search your literature for insight into baffling questions concerning your life. Nevertheless, for some, one's writing viewed as the primary window to their "interior world," is insufficient. They simply want the facts—more *scientific* evidence.

I am satisfied that neither I nor any of us will ever be fully knowledgeable of your most personal life because you were more a private person than your public image would suggest. Your life was distinctly different, in many ways, from the lives of most women of your era, particularly women of color. Courage and self-assurance were required as you stood in the shadow of mainstream literary tradition, ignoring the directive to keep a woman's place of silence and darkness. But your resistance was not without penalty. A woman pays handsomely for stepping outside the boundaries of the social space invisibly marked, "women only." One such space is that of the *unmarried* woman; she remains a social apparition and the spectacle. And disclaimers to the contrary, "intelligence" is considered another counter-feminine attribute. Your *intelligence* and failure to settle with one man targeted you for *criticism* and for *erasure*.

In the section "Love" in *Dust Tracks* you comment on whether women always keep their own counsel when it comes to discussing love: "Don't look for me to call a string of names and point out chapter and verse. Ladies do not kiss and tell any more than gentlemen do" (Wall 743).

What I am reaching for is a way to say that no matter whether you "told" or did not, in the larger sense, the nature of the literary products of your imagination convey who you are; they are your identity. For the imagination is the center of creative writing. Imagination linked with memory establishes, in breadth and depth, the essence of our dreams and the colors of our horizons.

The worlds that you created in fiction were first formulated in your childhood fantasy. You dreamed of what you would become at an early age and set out to make the dream the reality. In the opening lines of the novel *Their Eyes Were Watching God* you write "The dream is the truth. . . ." The relationships and associations that we form either make our dreams larger or they form roadblocks. An important aspect of the process of deciding whether to dream large or small is contingent upon the reservoir of inspiration carried over from the environment of our youth. Obviously yours was an enriching environment, an enclosure that held a generous portion of encouragement, moving you toward self-actualization.

Researchers have conducted studies that aim to ferret out the elements that make the critical developmental difference between those who evolve as full, life-loving, life-giving individuals and those who either become sociopathic, or simply are unable to self-actualize. Many of those who neither self-actualize nor are creative are those who experienced deprivation in their fantasy worlds as young children. Children whose parents are nurturing tend to more *easily* develop themselves and are more likely to become productive than are children of less nurturing parents.

In this context I raise questions that are critical to the assessment of the phrase, "Black womanhood." That you wrote essays, novels, ethnographies and plays, and collected folklore during a historical era that demanded something quite different from this of women, particularly, Black women, I find strikingly phenomenal. The evidence of your life, and I speak here of literary evidence, infers that you consistently challenged notions of the nature and substance of Black womanhood, a posture that placed you among a small group of Black, female writers and thinkers. I would not necessarily attribute your difference to *planned resistance* to social norms. Rather, it seems that you rejected the social norms established for women. Backgrounds differ widely among Black women. For example, *the culture* of your youth was supportive and quite divergent from the culture of my youth, despite our common African ancestry and despite the fact that we have the same gender. You grew up in a small, Black, southern town, while my youth was spent in a major northern city. As Black women, both your parents and mine experienced the limitations inherent in living in a racialized society. Yet the consequences, the related outcomes and impacts on our lives are quite disparate. The world of your reality and the world view out of which you carved fictional characters were shaped by unique regional elements such as folktales containing Black heroic figures, and, most important, Black governance was the community norm. It seems to me that the contours of my imagination still bare the imprint of northern racialization and the apartheid that I experienced. Mental decolonization is a life-long project for me.

The highly uncertain socioeconomic climate that you negotiated as a young woman and your progressive ideas on women's roles point towards extraordinary influences in the formation of the ethnic and gender identity found in your literature. I find small evidence of design and intent in the way you challenged the social order in fiction and essays. In your unofficial role of one literary foremother to contemporary Black women writers these attributes are especially meaningful. While we face race and gender barriers, your generation made our survival in the literary marketplace possible. Black women who write prose fiction and poetry such as Toni Morrison, Alice Walker, the late Toni Cade Bambara, Gwendolyn Brooks, and Paule Marshall are examples of some who follow your lead and whose work cuts across the grain of mainstream literary propriety. They provide major contributions to the Black literary canon and to the larger body of Western literature. Literary critics, essayists, polemicists, and cultural critics such as bell hooks, Hortense Spillers, and Karla F. C. Halloway are sharply analytical, and invoke powerful voices from their inner visions.

Of course the problem is that there are countless silent Black women. All of the writers I mention are richly talented. Many of those who are silent are also talented but lack a sense of agency, space, and empowerment. Central to your work and to that of the women named above, is their "telling" of our history bound up in sagas and analyses, in novels and critical essays. Yes, Black women fiction writers do write a history bound up in the stories of our circumstance and condition and presented through personal lenses. The absence of an authentic, documented history of our experience in the West, written in our own words, is a chasm which continues to be filled with the works of these and other such women. Others' work may also frame that experience or explore where we are and from where we have come, but we must fill in the blanks and rearrange the emphasis, add vital missing information and recreate the obscured texts of our lives. Our task is often corrective and creative literary productions that reinscribe the traditions of our foremothers.

You were the daydreaming young girl who climbed and lay in the arms of the Chinaberry tree and imagined yourself exploring the horizon to the end of the world. In womanhood the facility for fiction writing and storytelling for which you are known was primed in the flexing of the practice of daydreaming in the early years. Memory bound to the craft of writing gives us a gendered, energized, and culturally dense fiction. The youthful daydreams, I contend, are the creative force that later becomes a road map for the mature woman. You added immeasurably to your own writing pleasure by consciously moving between present, past, and future. But imagination and memory were joined to intensely motivate you and provide agency for your creative productivity. Your woman-voice is your own; uniquely resonant, pitched, colored, and intoned by internal and external worlds, worlds that are situated in a special cultural context.   .

Women's voices are interesting *instruments* of coded meaning and have extraordinary uses across cultures. An interesting example of woman's voice as instrument and one with which I am familiar is the voice of the Kayapo Indian woman in her Amazon Basin habitat in Brazil. Kayapo women use their voices in an unusual ritualistic manner known to outsiders as "keening." "Keening" is characterized by an excited, high-pitched, piercing sound, typically related to ritual practices that are a part of Kayapo life. One occasion in which women keen is during the young men's rite which requires that these young men climb tall trees in the forest. These trees have a proliferation of hornets' nests at their tops. The young men are repeatedly stung by the hornets as they reach the apex of their respective tree and must quickly shinny down to the ground, writhing in pain, pain that they must not acknowledge by crying out. It is the young men's mothers' role to "keen" as they remove hornets from their sons' bodies. Kayapo women also "keen" under other ritual conditions for which this gendered auditory practice, or vocalese, has different meanings (Cf. Turner, *Kayapo*).

I draw a parallel between "keening" Kayapo women and the poetics of your fictional women whose voices are also coded and have a multiplicity of meanings that may well escape comprehension outside a specific cultural context. For instance, the deeper, intrinsic meaning of Lucy Potts Pearson's voice as instrument might escape the culturally unfamiliar in the passage in *Jonah's Gourd Vine* where she talks about the meaning of the spider on the wall. Lucy's voice belongs to the personal and cultural nuances that influenced the lives of women as women and women in relationships with their men. This is one example of the way your writing emanates from a culturally conditioned female consciousness.

Your mother seemed to understand you and your vivid imagination and she spoke for you in situations where you could not speak for yourself. She was your protector and, I believe, much more. Lucy extended your reach towards the extraordinary and inferred that gender should not be used as a crutch nor an excuse for failure to achieve your dreams. Dreams, she suggests, are wise life investments. This is an important message that you provide in *Dust Tracks*.

No doubt, much of what your mother once dreamed of becoming was savored in her manner of relating to you. Your reports suggest that she invested something special in you, while shaping your female sensibility. Yes, mothers do that. When others threatened you and your world in any discernible way, Lucy intervened. You were nurtured and strengthened by her presence and took to heart the dictum she issued to all of her children: "jump at the sun" (572). The witness of your mother's enormous potential and equally of her suffering, perhaps mandated . . . dared you to be a different woman. Instructions such as these suggest that, perhaps, she had not. Nevertheless Lucy's unhappiness neither drove her to disinterest in her children nor to insanity; she survived.

Just as you internalized your mother's adage, "jump at the sun," contemporary Black women writers and non-writers identify with you and your life and struggle to write their world through your example. Because you are Black and female, your writing is especially meaningful for us. Lucy Hurston taught through direction, example, and thoughtful insinuation. Through her life you observed practical and useful lessons that have been passed on to us. One of those lessons is related to your view of Black women's suffering as redemptive. Janie, of *Their Eyes*, for example, is redeemed.

Lucy was the first and most meaningful image of Black womanhood that you knew. She suffered in the relationship with your father, John. While he was impressed by her poise and intelligence, he caused her pain. And we know that her death caused you to face amorphous shapes of horror and, for the first time, a sense of displacement. I believe that the grief and sense of displacement you felt then were fundamental in shaping your public personae and politics, and defining the parameters within which you would metamorphose and rename yourself, "Black woman" and "writer." Lucy's death then, I would suggest, significantly altered your life. No longer was she physically present, but you psychically recreated her through memory, fantasy, and imagination. Likewise, many Black women who read your work learn that suffering can teach resilience and should not become an excuse for malaise and life-long despair. In *Jonah's Gourd Vine*, Lucy Pearson (Hurston) is immortalized and continues to provide wisdom for women long after her death.

Doubtless women of color need the wisdom and practicality taught by our mothers and their mothers, for we are constantly challenged despite their history of valor and our own. Yes . . . in many ways your life was distinctly different from those of most women of your era. Only through conviction and self-assurance, gained early, could you write against mainstream tradition, paying little attention to the social pressure that would force you to keep a Black woman's designated place of silence and darkness. Resistance is not without penalty.

Today, the climate appears softer and more accepting of Black women at all levels of the social world. Yet, realistically, many of us live lives planned by others; and many are abused. Still we push the boundaries by asking questions, by naming ourselves: Black woman writer, teacher, mother, filmmaker, minister, healer, sister, daughter. You, and those before you have taught us well.

Hear the sound of my voice . . .
ride the breath of the wind

This Is About Somebody's Sun . . .

Nearly everyone with a genuine interest in Zora's life and work knows by now that she was born in Notasulga, Macon County, Alabama. Those with less serious interest probably believe that Eatonville, Florida was her birthplace. My reading of Zora's reaction to this generation's interest in that she is overwhelmingly surprised by it. She was at first surprised and uneasy because of all the rather sudden interest stirred up about her. But because she has now heard the Old Hag's voice crackling and half-singing she is at ease. The Old Hag sang one word but that became a song: "Nyazema." She heard it—Zora heard it over and over, again and again. The Old Hag's song searched everywhere and found her. She must have heard the word—the voice calling— "Nyazema" and it compelled her to reflect on her life, to think long and hard about it. The sound of the voice moved Zora to tears and created a sense of melancholy that urged her to recall the past. And although she might have appeared to be a very public woman, she was really quite private. Zora's age is an example of the private woman who lopped ten years off her age. Indeed, nearly every word she ever wrote or spoke is under a spy glass. She might just as well admit it—admit the lie she used to tell about her age. She was older than they thought. On January 7, 1891, they turned her out of her nice warm sauna into this often cold, unaccommodating, but fascinating world. It was a sink or swim proposition from the very beginning, and she always enjoyed a good swim, even in rough, choppy water.

I am sure she wants to tell you how much pleasure it gives her to know that the daughters and sons of Africa are so involved in probing the messages that she often hid in her books. And although she was not convinced that interest in her work would ever surface, there is a certain relief in knowing that her words inspire investigation. Modern research on the work she produced is affirming and might add to the efforts to revise and reinterpret early Black culture and history—topics that were always deeply interesting to her.

She wanted to talk about Black women, though. She always believed it important that a woman speak for herself and interpret events in her life as she lived them. No one else can do that. Through the consciousness of her fictional heroines, she attempted to show their inner wisdom as the major connection to events in their lives, whether or not they controlled those events. They were not wooden caricatures of women nor were they puppets. Her intent was to imbue them with a consciousness of themselves, and their history—their internal and external environments. These connections were important for their lives. There is special meaning in linking Black women, as a specific group within the African American community, to the traditions and values of Africa. She was aware that those linkages in her work were not always well received, and their intent often overlooked. For instance, it is important for Black women to know that West African women participate in a centuries old economic system. This does not mean that Black women in the African Diaspora would metamorphose over night, and become wealthy, but this knowledge might subtly influence what Black women believe to be possible, and might encourage them to dream out of historical experience . . . to connect with it.

Speaking of economics, she never sold more than five thousand of any of the books she wrote, including *Their Eyes Were Watching God*, Janie Mae Crawford's intriguing story. The characteristics of the reading public have changed since 1936 when she wrote *Their Eyes*. Many social movements—particularly the Civil Rights Movement of the 1960s and 1970s have heightened the political awareness of the average Black reader. And, as you know, Black womanhood has, by its very nature, political and economic implications.

You raise a concern of real substance for her—that is, (how to say this?), how might she define the most important aspects of Black womanhood? This is a topic she wrestled with in one way or another, in nearly all of her novels and records in folklore collections. She approached the topic from several angles, and said that the definition—more importantly, the meaning—of Black womanhood could not be settled either here or in any single place, for its meanings are many, and change over time. But there are basic aspects of Black womanhood that are directly related to our role as culture bearers. The core of her thought on this subject is folded within the personality and vision of her heroine, Janie Mae Crawford. She traveled to Haiti, to the Île de la Gonâve, to write the novel and, amazingly, completed it in seven weeks.

That book was borne of frustration, and bound up emotion, the result of a relationship she had recently ended and, she believed, threatened to dissolve her identity. She was compelled to find a way to reclaim herself; to balance her life again. It seemed a matter of sheer survival: freeing herself from a man who held a death grip on her heart and spirit. She was sinking into an abyss of vulnerability. Losing herself, totally, was something she could ill afford. The world might never fully appreciate the meaning of that relationship except through Janie's interaction with the men in *Their Eyes*. Especially telling is Janie's relationship with Tea Cake, and the inevitable, unexpected dissolution of their life together.

In *Their Eyes* she sketches a picture of her lost relationship with lines clear enough to reveal the pain and joy that she experienced in love. Whether to offer her whole life to the man she loved, or sacrifice the writing that she was so deeply committed to was the decision she painfully confronted. Because of her passion for both—the man and the work—like Janie, she would ultimately suffer the weight of either decision. Her work was her life, and to give it up seemed unbearable. There is the pain that one can tolerate, and then there is death. If she could not write then death was imminent. Death would come when she could no longer write. Having both the man and the work was not an option because he was unable to share her with her work. He viewed her writing as a distraction. She was deliciously flattered to know that she had a man who refused to share her with anything or anyone! But, as Nanny advises Janie Mae in *Their Eyes,* love can be an entrapment, a snare that catches many women. Perhaps for some women, there are other threats to their relationship—not the threat of a craft, such as writing. The threat can be nearly anything woman-fulfilling or time-consuming. The critical question that she faced was whether to live or die. That was the issue. Sound serious? It was serious. Whether to save her life or sacrifice herself to save him, the man she loved. The dictates of society would demand the latter.

He could not envision her attention devoted to anything other than himself. It was all too threatening. What is interesting is that she was writing throughout the life of the relationship! Trying to understand why she should not have the luxury of loving him, passionately, and making her art was deeply painful and frustrating. Janie's last moments with Tea Cake characterize that emotional conundrum—the forces of love and passion versus the will to survive.

In retrospect, it is clear that her early life experiences provided a preview of what it meant to face this type of dilemma. A dilemma in which the available choices force one to consider how to go on living in the face of fear and the loss of an abiding love. When her mother died, she was forced to deepen her capacity for self-direction, and for creative thinking. She called it "thinking for the sake of survival." But the capacity for creating a new reality and altering an existing one through her imagination had always been a strength. As a young girl she created stories and daydreamed whenever she wanted to feel peaceful about all kinds of situations. This habit followed her into adulthood. The point is that the soil of her youthful imagination, in part her own nature, in part the result of observing human imaginations always in motion, set the stage—lights and camera—for the drama on printed page. By that I mean that the stage was set . . . the verbal virtuosity of community orators that she observed as a child, embellishing, and repeating tales and "lies." Just as that "ritual" made life easier for them, she learned to depend on a powerful imagination to rescue her from despair. Her imagination was like a good sister she could call on in difficult times and could simply enjoy in others.

Her mother's death was followed by a long period of distress, familial disruption, and by the trauma of physical and psychological displacement. Ultimately, she enrolled in Morgan Academy, and, later, Howard University. Howard was important to her work because she had the opportunity to study under the Black master linguist, Dr. Lorenz Dow Turner, whose special research interest was Sea Island dialect, or "Gullah" language and culture. The language, the people, and the culture are known as "Gullah." The Sea Islands, of which there are many, are located off the East coast of South Carolina and Georgia. "Gullah" is a shortened form of the word, "Angola," the country in Africa from which many of the enslaved in the region were taken. Some call the "Gullah" "Geechees," and say that they speak "Geechee" language. But they actually speak an African language, modified by English! The Sea Island "Gullah" were, way back when, slaves who were isolated from the U. S. Mainland population. They were a kind of experiment. The story of the "Gullah" is a long and interesting one.

Another dilemma that she faced time and again in the 1920s and 1930s was the gulf between her desired life, and the prototype others held of an appropriate life for a Black woman. You raise that issue? When she arrived in New York in 1924, she had already learned that she could not separate herself from writing, not in any real sense. It was a part of her identity, and she was willing to work hard at her craft, placing no restrictions on herself because of gender—what a woman should *not* do. She was physically strong and had had brothers to tussle with in her youth, and so she never felt the need for "protection." More than that, adventure appealed to her—the child and the woman. She easily picked up her belongings, moving from one part of the country to another, and later lived outside the U. S. for extended periods—in Jamaica, Haiti, and British Honduras, collecting material for *Tell My Horse,* one of her works of folklore. Much of a woman's vulnerability, she believed, was not so much physical as psychological. Young girls internalize subtle but complex cultural values and messages; they are taught pliability, vulnerability, and care giving. Not often are they given messages that impart self-value. The challenge, she believes, is, first of all to value them, and then to convey that message to them and others.

In the fall of 1925, Zora enrolled at Barnard in anthropology, under Franz Boas ("Papa," as he was affectionately known.) Her studies with Boas provided the method for categorizing and structuring the stories and tales that she knew were abundant in the South—stories that she would later collect and have published. Particularly interesting were the stories she heard as a child in Eatonville, Florida. She was driven to make a go of her life, even if Black women were not supposed to do so. At Barnard, she was the only Black student in her classes.

About the time Charles Johnson published her short story, "Drenched in Light," in *Opportunity,* around 1924, she had high hopes that she would become a successful writer. She had had another short story, "John Redding Goes to Sea," and a poem, "O Night," published in Howard's literary club magazine, Stylus, in 1921. Anyway, she was confident in her chance for success. She met important literary figures in Harlem—people like Langston Hughes, Jean Toomer, Georgia Douglas, and Jesse Fauset. Women were always expected to walk a tightrope, and to function, more or less, as subordinate to their male counterparts. Acting at anyone's direction, other than one's own, she believed, would create problems over the long term. It was a matter of one's expectations for oneself. Contemporary views and protocols for women have shifted significantly, but only because women themselves have challenged history and ideas concerning their "proper" place.

Reading literature that focuses on the lives of women is a composite lesson in self-value. We grow stronger by "listening" to the voices of women who have refused to be silenced, and do not choose silence. You see, these are two different realities—being silenced and refusing silence. Neither, she believes is "natural" to the female experience. Women's writing is filled with important illustrations of ways to search for and find one's voice. She emphasizes this point in *Their Eyes*, and shows how Pheoby responds, both emotionally and politically, to Janie's recapitulation of past experiences. Janie's memory of events that have occurred in her life, and her narration of them, is heard and internalized by her friend, Pheoby. Pheoby subsequently inscribes Janie's "voice" upon the slate of her own consciousness and reacts to this inscription by reassessing her own mirror image. Finally, and most important, Pheoby declares, "Ah done growed ten feet higher from jus' listenin' tuh you, Janie. Ah ain't satisfied wit mahself no mo'." Like Pheoby, other women can experience the trials and triumphs of their foremothers and sisters through their literary "voices," and transfer literary lessons from the printed page onto the female consciousness. This is the potential for empowerment that is inherent in reading other women's words and hearing their voices. Other women's stories, both written and spoken, have the power to transport their "listeners" across common barriers, and to move women into themselves as free spirits.

Writing is not without sacrifice. We know that most Black women writers engage in their craft at great sacrifice, and the sacrifice may be either a personal relationship or a loss of financial stability. But by engaging the craft we assume the unfinished business of our foremothers and create a space for ourselves. Surrogate literary mothers and foremothers exist through whom ancestral voices speak to the young and impressionable. Theirs are voices of wisdom that offer strategies for resolving our prob-

lems. They suggest alternative social practices and ways of expe-
riencing the world. Important, too, are the contextual alignments
and revisions of history that Black women's writing produces. To
understand the words and place of other Black women, historically and in cultural context, is to strengthen and empower them
to scrutinize history for answers to hard questions about struggle.

Anthropology is the discipline . . . the field of Zora's training,
but history and its ancillary studies fascinated her—especially, the
history of religions. She had a deep interest in and knowledge
about religion, in part, because of her father's ministry. In *Moses,
Man of the Mountain*, she expresses that interest. In that work
she immerses Moses in a rural culture, and a cultural linguistics
of the Black South—the New World ancestral homeland of Blacks
in America. She gestures toward Africa as "mother," and progenitor of human life on the planet, Earth. As she does so, she
honors the notion of "foremother," "mother," as antecedant (not
necessarily the biological edict of woman as "mother"). Reference to Africa as ancestral homeland appears elsewhere in her
work, such as in the Everglades hurricane scene in *Their Eyes*.
Lias, a minor character, leaves for an area of safety, as he tells
Jane and Tea Cake, "I'll see you in Africa." Focusing her attention
on Africa was not particularly advantageous, in the political sense,
for as has been noted,

> The fiction of the Negro (Harlem) Renaissance was predominantly a
> middle-class fiction. There was a "genteel school" of which most Black
> women writers were a part: Georgia Douglas Johnson, Jessie Fauset,
> Anne Spencer and Angelina Grimke are representative of that literary
> persuasion. Works rendered in African-American folk tradition, by
> women, were an anomaly. (*Cavalcade* 416)

Frankly speaking, Black southern folk-language was an embarrassment for many of her associates. She understood very clearly
that this was a double historic period, with the war and the pro-
fusion of Black music, art, and literature. Black men had only
recently returned from World War I that had cost many lives. The
sacrifices made by Black soldiers and their families. . . . These
were men who returned to America and brought with them a
searing need for radical social change and justice. They believed
that there should be retribution for Blacks who would never return, who sacrificed their lives in the theater of war. These men's

beliefs were strongly felt by some in the literary community situated in Harlem. They knew that Black soldiers died with honor, and believed that Black Americans had earned their right to live with dignity. For some writers, however, dignity meant a denial of Black folk tradition. She thought of Lorenzo Dow Turner's research on the "Gullah." Yes! Dr. Turner's work emphasized the importance of particularized language systems as cultural markers. Indeed, Blacks should have all of the rights of citizenship without having to "prove" anything to so-called "high culture."

To the surprise of a number of her contemporaries, she believed that Blacks were neither intrinsically "downtrodden" nor "tragic." For her, Black life was inaccurately depicted as "tragedy," because she had no childhood memories that reflected a people who faced life's challenges as "tragedy." Tragedy simply was not a remembered dominant childhood theme. That is not to deny her keen awareness of racial problems and injustice, but her youth was inherently rich, even in its material simplicity.

The woman we know as Zora Hurston aimed to write fiction in a manner that would acknowledge the existence of race prejudice in the lives of Blacks, yet she would characterize Black resistance to oppression through valorous Black folktales, short stories, and other evidence of historical and contemporary cultural viability. A Black readership would not be forced to recoil, or to harbor feelings of deep hopelessness. In other words, collecting Black folklore and writing fiction reflected her awareness of "race," and the meaning of "difference," without the political didacticism that she would later reveal in articles and essays such as "The Pet Negro System (1943)," and "Negroes Without Self Pity (1943)," or "Crazy for This Democracy (1945)," and "What White Publishers Won't Print (1950)." In these early days, she believed that fictional emphasis on culture and tradition, folk language, and an inferred philosophical perspective was an effective means to enhancing esteem for Blacks in America. She once stated her belief that we Blacks needed "new words" to express ourselves and our culture. Thus, the spatial separation of White, Maitland, Florida, from the all-Black Eatonville of her youth was not experienced as a disadvantage.

She speaks of the sentiments expressed by some Blacks in the 1950s and 1960s that strongly favored school integration as an equal education opportunity for their children—a sentiment which she did not share. She opposed integration as a viable solution to Black children's educational disadvantage. This was an opinion for which she was severely criticized. Her interest lay in self-appreciation for all races; lacking as she did the "victim" mind set which plagued some of her Harlem contemporaries. After all, she was acclimated to Black leadership, because she grew up observing it, for her father was also Mayor of the town.

During the early years in Eatonville she did not observe her family, friends, or neighbors remorsefully weighing and lamenting their social condition on the scale of humankind because of their race. She was not politically naive. One might say that many Black folktales are dramatizations of individual and collective Black political resourcefulness, and the capacity to overcome misfortune, even to enjoy life in its adversity. These stories show that Blacks have both the will and the ingenuity to overcome oppression. Black folk culture suggests that Whites may have social and economic privilege, but Blacks have the philosophical, spiritual, cultural, and creative edge. This edge assumes the form of a zest for life and laughter, an entrenched fortitude, and a rich heritage, worthy of preservation and perpetuity.

Her first novel, *Gourd Vine*, reflects the cultural characteristics of an Eatonville childhood; its joys and sorrows. Most importantly the novel depicts a particular Black community's consciousness of itself in space and time. The first mental images of the novel took form in 1929. She mentions the concept of the novel's form in her autobiography, *Dust Tracks*:

> While I was in the research field in 1929, the idea of *Jonah's Gourd Vine* came to me. I had written a few short stories, but the idea of attempting a book seemed so big, [I] hid it away from even myself . . . . For one thing, it seemed off-key. What I wanted to tell was a story about a man, and from what I had read and heard, Negroes were supposed to write about the Race Problem. I was and am thoroughly sick of the subject. My interest lies in what makes a man or a woman do such-and-so, regardless of his color. It seemed to me that the human beings I met reacted pretty much the same to the same stimuli . . . . But I said to myself that was not what was expected of me, so I was afraid to tell a story the way I wanted, or rather the way the story told itself to me. So I went on that way for three years. (Wall 713)

Gourd Vine lived in her, quieted by a fear of social criticism and censure. We are often so fearful of consequences that the idea of self-expression smothers. Many female voices are often not heard because of the presence of such fear. Societal erasure

of women's roles in history, coupled with their fear of disapproval
paralyzes many, both mind and hand. She reminds you that these
are learned behaviors and, therefore, are alterable! Reflecting
again on the Eatonville of her youth, she recalls some of the
women who lived by lowering their eyelids and pulling down the
shade of life on themselves. They were bound tightly by the roles
into which tradition placed them—a tradition that limits women's
humanity and participation in the drama of life should be up-
rooted and banished to Earth's outer limits. In *Their Eyes*, we see
in Janie Mae Crawford one woman's insistence on "choice"
graphically depicted. Janie is the portrait of a woman who must
give and receive love. Desire is clearly a part of Janie's psyche,
yet she establishes parameters for the expression of that desire.
For this reason, and others, Janie is faced with community disapproval and verbal reprisal.

Janie Mae Crawford walked away from Logan Killicks, her first
husband, and buried Jody Starks, her second. There were many
times when she might have had other relationships, were she not
holding on to the vision of herself as deserving of a "good" man;
the man of her dreams. The second mate in the novel, Jody Starks
whom she survives, thrives on ridicule and demeaning comments
about his wife, Janie. Jody was particularly caustic in his remarks
about her advance into middle-age. For Jody, Janie was no longer
a "young pullet," and ought to have conducted herself in the
manner of the old woman he believed her to be. Jody's desire
was that Janie internalize his assessment of her as "stupid," a
belief that he held about all women. In short, Jody declared psychological warfare against his wife, and taunted her relentlessly.
In a particularly salient exchange, Zora attempts to show Janie's
consciousness, and her will to self-rule. At last, returning her
husband's insults in the company of others she commands him
to "Stop mixin' up mah doings wid mah looks . . . Jody. When
you get through tellin' me how tuh cut uh plug uh tobacco, then
you kin tell me whether mah behind is on straight or not." Stunned
to hear Janie's forthright speech, Jody engages her in a battle of
verbiage, or signifying:

"Wha-whut's dat you say Janie? You must be out yo' head."
"Naw, Ah ain't outa mah head neither."
"You must be. Talkin' any such language as dat."

"You de one started talkin' under people's clothes. Not me."

"Whut's de matter wid you, nohow? You ain't no young girl to be gettin'
all insulted 'bout yo' looks. You ain't no young courtin' gal. You'se uh
ole woman, nearly forty."

"Yeah, Ah'm nearly forty and you'se already fifty. How come you can't
talk about dat sometimes instead of always pointin' at me?"

"T'ain't no use in gettin' all mad, Janie, 'cause Ah mention you ain't no
young gal no mo'. . . ." (Wall 237–38)

Unapologetically, Janie owns her middle-age, and summarily
wounds Jody to the core of his being with the weaponry of powerful words:

Naw, Ah ain't no young gal no mo' but den Ah ain't no old woman
neither. Ah reckon Ah looks mah age too. But Ah'm uh woman, every
inch of me, and Ah know it. . . . You big-bellies round here . . . but 'tain't
nothin' to it but yo' big voice. Humph! Talkin' 'bout me lookin' old!
When you pull down yo' britches, you look lak de change uh life. (238)

The internal image that Janie holds of herself will not permit
self-betrayal. If one looks at Janie's grandmother, Nanny, and her
definition of Black womanhood, it is clearly at odds with Janie's.
They clash most directly when Janie is forced by a sense of responsibility to Nanny to marry Logan Killicks, a man who in no
way evokes her desire. Nanny's influence is symbolic, for it is not
unusual for a woman to do what Janie is expected to—to toss
aside her dreams in order to satisfy others. Janie adheres to
Nanny's wish, and marries Logan Killicks, later discovering a bitterness toward her grandmother. About Janie's thoughts, Zora
wrote:

She hated her grandmother and had hidden it from herself all these
years under a cloak of pity. . . . Here Nanny had taken the biggest thing
God ever made, the horizon . . . and pinched it in to such a little bit of a
thing that she could tie it about her granddaughter's neck tight enough
to choke her. She hated the old woman who had twisted her so in the
name of love. Most humans didn't love one another nohow, and this
mis-love was so strong that even common blood couldn't over come it
all the time. (138)

Nanny's role in Janie's life may be viewed, metaphorically, as a
composite sketch of several social forces. For Janie, love and desire were at the center of the universe. Having narrowed her universe to satisfy someone else, Janie felt profound deprivation.

Zora also uses Logan Killicks and Jody Starks symbolically, for they represent the value placed on Black women in society. They are novelistic personifications that show the twisted and distorted view of society towards the Black woman—servants and agents of the desires of others.

So you ask, "What is Black womanhood?" It seems the longer she ponders the question, the less sure she is of where to place the emphasis. But she knows that every view is subjective. Emphasis is the issue, the focus. Her emphasis, her sense of things may be politically divergent. But she does not skirt it, because she believes that listening to one another's views assures diverse perspectives, cross-referential definitions and broadened visions. Diversity serves the good of the whole.

First, she believes that as women of African heritage, we would be wise to consider the collective good. She means as far as decisions about what is in our best interest is concerned. For example, she thinks that writers should write; non-writers should assist them in making that possible, or at least not stand in their path. The form of our collective consciousness is another important consideration. When she says, "collective consciousness," she means that there is a need to work single-mindedly around concerns such as protection of ourselves against any and all forms of violence, particularly, violence towards our children. Children must be central . . . protected. Black women should learn to recognize abuse, for it assumes the form of a thief who, in the dark of night, steals your pride and dignity. Such verbal abuse, for example, as Janie Mae suffers from some men in *Their Eyes*, is violence. That's her judgment. Lucy Pearson in *Gourd Vine* is also abused by her husband, John. These are crimes perpetrated within the community. And societal abuse includes everything from forced silence and distorted visual images, to poor health care, and quasi-medical practices, such as "policing the Black woman's body" around issues of fertility and child-bearing. When women openly discuss and write about these and other concerns, even in fictive form, there is the potential for appropriating comfort, peace, joy, and security.

She suspects that those Black women who step out, and honor their inner voices, who validate and value themselves publicly and privately, will suffer intense feelings of fear, apprehension and possibly experience retribution. Unfortunately, internalized oppression often causes other women to refuse to come to our aid in times of trouble. Their communication is strained and strident. Working towards creative support for others like yourselves is to guard against the satirical images you often experience. Black womanhood, then, encompasses several levels of consciousness—consciousness of your difference and similarity, and of your relationships with others. You ought to strive to be your true selves, for authenticity is the only basis for building bridges. Although not always acknowledged, the destiny of women of color has always been linked, globally; another reality with which you ought to come to terms. She knows that great strides have been made in that direction. Having travelled widely and living among geographically dispersed Black populations, she can say to you that the social worlds of women of color are similarly circumscribed across cultures. Put another way, Black womanhood is also a global space of political consciousness of one's self in relation to others. Black womanhood is, then, in part, acknowledgment of the implications of difference, in a race- and gender-conscious world.

She felt disconnected in many ways from other Black women writers at the apex of her career; therefore, a majority of her associates, male and female were White. She regrets that she shared few enduring relationships with other Black women. Women tend to view other women as enemies, and are threatened rather than strengthened by their presence. Much of this distrust is attributable to the limit placed on the number of Blacks, generally, and women, particularly, who will be free. The sports arena may be the exception, because it is so non-threatening to the existing social order. Sports, as entertainment, also provides a broad financial base in this society, and enables other enterprises. As for academe, it is the polar opposite of sports; it is characterized by limitation and contested access to any real power for Blacks.

She trusts that Janie Mae Crawford reaches readers as the multidimensional Black woman of her inner vision. It must be difficult to write the character in the way one "feels" her. Think of Janie as a skeletal frame that we might build on Black woman-flesh. As you might observe, Janie is her mirror image, in many ways. But she is also her antithesis. Although conscious of herself and her desire, in early relationships Janie is defined by men because Nanny privileged security rather than love and self-value. It is all right by Nanny that Logan Killicks is neither loved nor desired by Janie: he has forty acres under plow, and a house. Nanny's position is one that she comes to from many deeply bitter experiences. Most outstanding among them is the abuse suffered at her "Mistis'" hand, the rape by her "Master," and the rape of her daughter, Janie's mother, Leafy, by her White school teacher. The rape of Leafy dissolves Nanny's dreams for her, and totally undermines Leafy's own human potential.

Symbolically, Janie's story also portrays the meaning of women's relationships, and their power to contribute to one another's emotional and psychic growth; the power to transform one another. She also attempts to show the critical role "words" and "listening" play in life. Both *telling* and *hearing* are critical "performances," for they engage and expand you, embody potential change, and create agency. "Telling" and "hearing"—these are interactions that rely on personal interpretation, analysis, and sense-making. The "storyteller" selects information to disclose, and creates the method of information transmission. The "listener(s)" filters the message through her complex web of categories of possible meanings, all the while choosing connections, and teasing out "implicit" and "intended" meanings. Janie's voice, her words, her story, are potent change agents which alter Pheoby's image of herself in the world and, therefore, rearrange existing strategies for Pheoby's life. One might read the meaning of these two women's "talk" as Pheoby Watson's initiation into the cult of "true Black womanhood."

Conversely, we hear other women's negative judgments and hurtful critiques that are often cast at Janie, like stones. One instance is the segment in *Their Eyes* where Janie returns to town after a period of two years' absence. She is the subject of petty ridicule by the townsfolk, male and female. The strongest and most damaging words come from other women. They are jealous of Janie's willingness to risk their criticism for the sake of living according to the dictates of her own heart, prevailing social expectations, notwithstanding. Janie's critics' narrowly circumscribed lives add to their hunger for the flesh of gossip:

What she doin' coming back here in dem overhalls? Can't she find no dress to put on?—Where's dat blue satin dress she left here in?—Where

all dat money her husband took and died and left her?—What dat ole
forty year ole 'oman doin' wid her hair swingin' down her back lak some
young gal?—Where she left dat young lad of a boy she went off here
wid?—Thought she was going to marry?—Where he left her?—What he
done wid all her money?—Betcha he off wid some gal so young she ain't
even got no hairs—why she don't stay in her class? (175–76)

Janie's intrepid behavior ignored class, which, in this instance,
should be interpreted to infer gender. In their collective role as
community guardians of the status quo, they also personify the
subversive attitudes and actions often demonstrated by women
toward one another. These attitudes emerge in situations where
one woman, among a group of peers, dares to trust and follow
her inner voice, a voice inaudible to the others. Her inner voice
may directly defy social expectations, particularly expectations
for Black women. In fact, the "unconventional" woman may well
provoke hard questions among her peers about the quality of
their lives. For Janie, Pheoby's true friendship contributes im-
mensely to Janie's ability to assess and work through her personal pain. Pheoby provides a fertile and therapeutic ear for Janie's
recapitulation of both painful and joyous events. The "talking"
"listening" therapy is a performance through which Janie reenacts
important events, benefitting both herself and Pheoby, "storyteller"
and "listener."

Like Janie who returns to town dressed differently, wearing
clothes judged inappropriate to her age and gender, Zora frequently was criticized because of her appearance—her style. The
deeper issue was always an expression of disapproval for a breach
of social protocol. These attitudes prevailed towards her public
personality and extended, often, to her writing. That she sometimes appeared in public places wearing trousers, therefore, often became grist for the gossip mill. She could ill afford more
than scant attention to social conventions of dress, for other "real"
issues (food, and shelter) demanded her meager earnings. Sometimes her shoes (and heart) even had a hole in them. Painfully, she
admits that financial insecurity also led to professional compromise,
meaning that she fought openly for the survival of her ideas, but
frequently had to live with the critical opinions of benefactors. Many
times they dictated what should, and what should not be included
in her projects. Both became loathsome; the financial lack and the
constant scrutiny of her writing by benefactors.

In the Harlem of the 1920s and 1930s the majority of patrons of the Black arts were wealthy White women. Few Black artists were ever self-supporting. Cultural difference and cultural value issues were faced by nearly all of the writers of the period with benefactors.

Political issues were difficult to resolve to the satisfaction of both writer and financier. Benefactors were, of course, often highly selective of the writing that they were willing to support, and occasionally, irreconcilable differences prevailed between the two points of view. Further, Black writers were sometimes forced to rationalize defection from important ideas that were linked to their craft in order to accommodate a benefactor's desires.

Zora was judged harshly by peers for the long patron-writer relationship that she maintained with Charlotte Osgood Mason. Much of the criticism, although cloaked in concern for the political ramifications of this relationship, was also a politics of gender. It is true, then, that only when a woman is self-supporting and independent is she able to speak and to write without fear. Who knows, who is to say what the literature of that period in Harlem might have been in a different economic climate?

Black womanhood . . . , "True Black womanhood?" There are prerequisites. It emerges only when a woman is financially secure in her own right. She fretted whenever she found herself in an un-equal relationship with anyone. Yet she was compelled to compete in a marketplace where women were both scarce and unwelcomed. Not only was she female; add to that, "unconventional" and a product of the South! These factors contributed to "irreconcilable" differences among some of her peers. Class. This could be an issue of class for some. You see, there was the drama of North versus South. Northern "high culture,"and the rural, unsophisticated "folk" of the South.

The point is that poverty forces compromise. Again, in *Their Eyes* she shows Nanny, a poor Black woman, forced to raise Janie in "the white folks' backyard." Janie is, of course, also poor. Nanny's and Janie's poverty and "objective" position—that of outsiders to the Washburns, the White family for whom Nanny works, deprives Janie of a *name*. An identifier. It tells who you are. Until she is six years old, Janie is known as "alphabet,"— a symbol to be arranged in any number of ways, and with alternate and dubious meanings . . . "'cause so many people had done

named me so many names." Namelessness portends the absence
of identity and the lack of self-definition. Poverty can, and does,
create namelessness, selflessness, and death. Zora was a Black
woman who yearned to write her way through life, and found
financial dependence to be a constant tear in the seam of personal wholeness. It was an identity issue. Who am I? To whom
do I belong? Maybe . . . just maybe, she even "performed" for
Whites.

Janie Crawford's youthful poverty did not undermine the development of sensitivity and intelligence in womanhood. For despite her desire for love, to give and receive it, she rejected de-
valuing, dehumanizing relationships constructed for the sake of
security. One might euphemistically call Janie a "work in
progress." And, in a real way, we should view our lives similarly.
But Janie was consciously determined to develop all of the aspects of herself. Through Janie Mae Crawford Zora also explored
a number of approaches to resolving conflict in a woman's life
and attempted to elucidate the heroine's interior consciousness
so that others might be inspired to ask questions of themselves,
and their lives. Many women have witnessed a "bad" relationship, if they have not experienced one. Logan Killicks, and Jody
Starks are prototypes and symbols of the consequences of mate-
riality. We understand Nanny's motive, but the outcome is painful and debilitating for Janie.

Try as she might, Nanny would not be moved from her vision
of Logan Killicks. For Janie, Killicks is disgusting: "He looks like
some ole skull head in de graveyard," she says. After Nanny recites an impressive list of sacrifices she has made for Janie, Janie
simply pouts. Nanny slaps Janie's face, then recognizing her own
suffering and the child's, she encourages Janie to sit on her lap
while she explains, apologetically, that her only desire is to see
that no harm should come to the girl. Nanny then offers her granddaughter a profound message:

> Honey, de white man is de ruler of everything as fur as Ah been able tuh
> find out. Maybe it's some place away off in de ocean where de black
> man is in power, but we don't know nothin' but what we see. So de
> white man throw down de load and tell de nigger man tuh pick it up. He
> pick it up because he have to, but he don't tote it. He hand it to his
> womenfolks. De nigger woman is de mule uh de world so fur as Ah can
> see. Ah been prayin' fuh it tuh be different wid you. Lawd, Lawd, Lawd!
> (186)

After their marriage Killicks begins to treat Janie with disdain, makes negative reference to her background and debases her for not showing the gratitude he feels he deserves. Janie soon becomes emotionally distant from her husband.

While Killicks is off one day buying a mule for Janie's use in plowing the fields, a strange man passes by the farm and sees her working. He is dressed all "citified," and asks for a cool drink of water, which Janie provides. This was her beginning with Jody Starks. He begins almost immediately boasting about the $300 he's saved up from working for White folks, and boldly announces that he is heading for a place in Florida where they are "makin' a town all outa colored folks."

Following their first encounter, Janie and Jody meet regularly in the scrub oaks adjacent to Killicks's farm. Despite her disappointment over the state of her marriage to Killicks, for a while Janie resists the temptation to exit the relationship, and attempts to forewarn Logan that another man is openly pursuing his interest in her. Killicks is simply unable to hear Janie's words of foreboding. It is here that she notes the importance of "new words." The day that Janie acts upon her decision to leave, we hear:

> The morning road air was like a new dress. That made her feel the apron tied around her waist. She untied it and flung it on a low bush beside the road and walked on, picking flowers and making a bouquet. After that she came to where Joe Starks was waiting for her with a hired rig. He was very solemn and helped her to the seat beside him. Her old thoughts were going to come in handy now, but new words would have to be made and said to fit them. (200)

Not only are new words important to the success of this union, Janie's new relationship is one based on *choice*. Zora viewed a woman's freedom to exercise choice to be central to her physical and spiritual harmony. She emphasizes the term, "new words" because existing language is not always suitable for the expression of new insight, new ideas, new conditions.

After seven years of marriage to Jody Starks, who becomes a spirit-squelching element in her life, Janie feels diminished. In Jody's view, she is inept and needs direction in every thought and action. He assigns her a place in his life, which is summed up in his response to a complaint Janie wages against his obtrusiveness. Janie warns Jody of the strain and unnaturalness placed on their relationship, the result of his over-valued position as Mayor of the town. Janie also complains about his frequent absence from home: "You'se always off talkin' and fixin' things, and I guess I feels lak Ah'm jus' markin' time."

Janie is more an appendage than a fulfilled woman. Zora drew out these passages to emphasize and illustrate points she believed to be connections in her fiction that, in their totality, painted pictures that responded to some women's issues. She did not choose them sequentially. Nevertheless, they created a vision of Hurston's woman-centered awareness across time. Jody's death provides the segue to Janie's third and most gratifying relationship.

Janie met Vergible Woods (Tea Cake) one evening at her grocery store, an inheritance from Jody. Tea Cake is a man obviously several years younger than she. He first gives the appearance of just meandering into the store. Tea Cake is a kind of drifter who exchanges kind words with Janie and engages her in a game of checkers one evening. Having longed to play the game, she is excited at this chance, for Jody held restrictions against such activity. Tea Cake's easy smile and manner cause Janie to feel that she has known him all of her life. No awkward uneasiness attends the opening ritual of their emergent relationship. She is curious about the man, and knows intuitively that somehow he is different from others she has known.

Janie is intrigued by Tea Cake because of the equalitarian attitude he displays towards her. She has longed for inclusion in some of the interesting, routine activities of her small community. The game of checkers fascinated her from a distance, as did the exchange of tales that occurred on her store's front porch. With Tea Cake, playing checkers is only the beginning of the rainbow. For the first time in her life Janie feels that she is viewed as a whole person, a woman who is *both* capable and interesting. Tea Cake and Janie become lovers and share many experiences—everything from working in the cane fields together to preparing breakfast for one another. Not uncharacteristic of intimate relationships, they fight and love alternately, not always aware of the end of one emotion and the other's beginning. Opportunity for self-expression is the important difference between Janie's relationship with this younger man, and marriage to either Logan Killicks or Jody Starks. Even in difficult times Janie can be open with Tea Cake. For example, she expresses bold anger and jealousy over what she fears might be a relationship between Tea Cake and another woman working in the sugar cane field. Janie believes that Tea Cake is lying about the issue. She first admits her pain: "You done hurt mah heart, now you come wid uh lie tuh bruise mah ears!. . . ." Ultimately,

> They wrestled on until they were doped with their own fumes and ema-
> nations; till their clothes had been torn away; till he hurled her to the
> floor and held her there melting her resistance with the heat of his body,
> doing things with their bodies to express the inexpressible; kissed her
> until she arched her body to meet him and they fell sleep in sweet ex-
> haustion. (287)

Zora's major aim in presenting Janie's three marriages is to raise the level of women's awareness of their potential as change agents in their own lives. Janie's marriages contextualize her dialog with Pheoby Watson. Therefore, while many critiques of *Their Eyes* focus on Janie's marriages, these unions might be viewed as secondary to Janie's "talking performance" for Pheoby. It is this latter interaction, the "telling" and "hearing" that become a ritual of healing for Janie and for Pheoby. Zora's own life lacked such deep sisterly relationships. This, then, is a message to women which suggests that relationships among them offer unparalleled opportunities for sharing and growth. For she believes that the mirror of reflection holds the possibility for creating a regenerative frame of mind. She attempted to create a mood in the mind of the reader, particularly the Black female reader, that might lead to examination of her inner self. As she grew older, the importance of inner harmony was notable and confirmed.

While Janie Mae Crawford may not be the prototypical Black woman in all respects, for Zora she represented the strength of will and the kind of tenacity needed by the Black woman who decides to manage her life consonant with the direction of her inner voice. Certainly, some aspects of Janie's life are reflections of the writer's. But like all women, Janie must be viewed in the context of her time and her space. She was a heroine in her day; an independent thinker. Although the plot speaks to the marginality of Black women and their social and political vulnerability, Janie's behavior is unusual. Vulnerability . . . that's what we see in Leafy, and in Leafy's mother, Nanny . . . that they lack control of their destiny. Janie engages life seeking change. She is the agent of change in her own life and in Pheoby Watson's.

Janie is also plagued by social concepts of *class*, first as a child who is maligned because she was "raised in the white folks' kitchen," later by her first husband, Logan, who believes he "saved" Janie by "takin' her in." Jody views maleness to be a superordinate class or caste superior to femaleness. Finally, the "porch sitters," those who, upon her return to town, attempt to sit in judgement of Janie, and suggest that she ought not to upset the social order, and "stay in her own class."

For Janie's creator, time and space, notwithstanding, as a character she embodies many elements of "true" Black womanhood; an artist's composite sketch. She is both the embodiment and negation of Zora Neale Hurston.

Sing the song of her primeval name . . .

Quarter Moon:
. . . In a Manner of Speaking

". . . Mah tongue is in mah friend's mouf."
Zora Neale Hurston, *Their Eyes Were Watching God*

I resonate with the thoughts you express, with your ideas. Yes, particularly with your discussion of the undervaluation of Black women in our society. This sentiment certainly holds for all of Black life, but here we focus on women. To some extent we also refer to the way that women's lives affect their children's—Nanny and Leafy, in *Their Eyes* are good examples, you know. This undervaluation shows through in so many ways—daily news in the media, all the way to the oral reports, and some of the scenarios in the folklore collections you published. The evidence proliferates the social world, and is global. On the positive side, this is also evidence in your work of great value placed on women, as opposed to devaluation. For example, you show that women are valued among rural Haitians, whose practices are recorded in the compilation of your field experiences, *Tell My Horse*. The Vodou priestesses of Haiti are an example of the value and power certain segments of African Diasporic peoples traditionally invest in women. As you learned through field interviews, observations, and conversations, clearly, philosophically and ritualistically, Haitians sanctify "femaleness." The outcome of one discussion that you record in *Tell My Horse* reveals the sanctity of womanhood within the context of a Haitian religious cosmology.

You report a discussion that you had in Haiti with a Dr. Holly. Dr. Holly posed a question that might be considered *rhetorical* by the culturally uninformed, but is one of importance for understanding a traditional Haitian view of women. In *Tell My Horse* you report that Dr. Holly asks the question: "What is the truth?" And you wrote:

> Knowing that I could not answer him he answered himself through a Voodoo
> ceremony in which the Mambo, that is the priestess, richly dressed, is asked
> this question ritualistically. She replies by throwing back her veil and reveal-
> ing her sex organs. . . . The ceremony means that this is the infinite, the
> ultimate truth. There is no mystery beyond the mysterious source of life. . . .
> The Mambo discards six veils . . . and falls . . . naked, intoxicated to the
> ground. It is considered the highest honor for all males participating to kiss
> her organ of creation, for Damballa, the god of gods has permitted them to
> come face to face with truth. (376)

Not surprisingly, in the light of slave cargoes to islands in the Atlantic Ocean, the value placed on women in much of traditional West
African culture is reflected in Haitians' obvious reverence for the mystery of creation which a woman's body represents. The ritual Dr. Holly
recites simply insinuates cultural acknowledgment of woman's mystery and power, concepts that rest at the core of Haitian cosmogony,
and ethereal worlds. A primary reason for my emphasis on Black
women's value in our conversation is that we nearly lost you and your
legacy to a junk heap of inferior writers. I wonder how many others,
like you, are hidden away, unheard of, and unheralded. You were a
near casuality of the "choose-between" games the powerful play with
Black Art and Black artists. "Choose-between," expresses the external nature of decisions made by others for Blacks and by those who
control access to Black cultural products. Many years passed during
which most of your work was out of print. Even after the 1960s Civil
Rights Movement, few university professors had ever heard your name.
With the more recent appropriation of Black cultural products—so
often for their economic value—popular culture, and the newest Black
literary renaissance, Zora Neale Hurston is a globally recognized name.

A review of the period in which you were most prolific portends
clues, social and political, to help us understand why your work was
so long "secreted" away. Forgotten. Two of your novels—*Moses, Man
of the Mountain* and *Their Eyes*—are particularly provocative for their
parallels with slave narratives. Like slave narratives, these novels call
to mind situations which many of your contemporaries, Black and
White, would rather have neither read nor discussed. Slave narratives,
you know, simultaneously mask and disclose. *Their Eyes* and *Moses*
are narrated in such a way that they disclose or chronicle the existence
of a vibrant cultural community of Black survivors from the institution
of slavery. These works, like slave narratives, are essentially, "confes-
sions" or "tales" of Black valor in the face of the most dire living
conditions to which humans have been subjected in recorded history.

In these novels and in slave narratives a community survives a set of artfully articulated conditions which separate them from Whites and codify their collective *identity* and their *difference* from Whites. Masked in your work is the process by which this communal richness sustains itself. Often the slave narrative masks through its use of pseudonyms, withholding the names of persons who aided a slave's escape or an insurrection. Slave narratives also often deny, in form and substance, the intensity of the author's commitment to a mission of liberation.

Already we have touched lightly upon some of the political factors that contributed to your near exile, but there are more layers of the social sediment that contributed to the "disappearance" of Zora Neale Hurston. The spirit or "will to survive" evidenced in your fictional women's lives—especially Janie in *Their Eyes* and Lucy, in *Jonah's Gourd Vine*, betray a particular world view, and orientation. You create vocal women—women of voice, against the grain of social expectation when women were expected to be greatful for any small opportunity to speak. Through female characters you also express personal thoughts and feelings and display regions of internal conflict universal among Black women. Some of these conflicts are related to ageism, such as was aimed at and heaped upon Janie Mae by the community in *Their Eyes*. And as a result of the early liberation of your imagination you freed yourself to create and resolve personal, social, and political problems through language. The new words that you call for in *Their Eyes*; "new words," that you wrote "would have to be made" to fit old thoughts tempered by time are emergent, as you show, in women's writing. Writing represents, on one level, your way of confronting the world. At another level your writing reveals a vast horizon of alternatives that would later prompt two generations of Black women to fashion and create "new words" to describe and alter their worlds. For as we read you, many of us consider what we must confront and resolve on the terrain of race, gender, and class.

This survivalist dimension of your persona accounts for, at least in part, the interest some of your peers showed in critiquing your personal conduct rather than your literature prior to the Civil Rights Movement of the 1960s. The race/gender combination embodied in your work did not, in the beginning endear you to a wide audience. I want to place the post Civil Rights Movement demands of Black students and their supporters at colleges and universities for inclusion of the Black experience in their curriculum in a line emerging from a Black literary and artistic aesthetic related to the movement. The Black Studies curriculum required an archaeology of Black literary products. Several Black women writers were discovered in this era for the first time, or discovered anew. Most participants in the movement met Zora Neale Hurston, then, for the first time. This meeting, the outgrowth of Black protest for revision of the social and historical framework of Americana, demanded another emphasis in the college curriculum, and later included Women's Studies. Many of these women, mostly White, also participated in the Civil Rights Movement, or were familiar with the strategies Blacks employed at its apex. Such strategies were used to an even greater advantage than was the case for Black Americans. These women enjoyed access to the publishing apparatuses of the society and quickly formed a broad and effective corpus of literature to support their political agenda. This was yet another means of access to your writing.

Your "New Negro" contemporaries sometimes demurred at images of "Negro" life rendered in your work, particularly those images for which you are now most widely praised, folk tradition and gender relations within Black culture. One could argue that your literary and real life politics made you a sitting duck for considerable rancor and criticism.

Importantly, you also show the cultural politics of language throughout most of your fictional work. Southern Black folk language, you remind us, is a particularized system of verbal communication which embodies a world view that holds a special place among its users: there is no embarrassment for a creolized form of English. The trend among many leaders and spokespersons of the Harlem Renaissance was toward a White, male-dominated literary model. In fact, you were associated with the more radical fringe of Harlem's literary community. I would say that *Fire,* the short-lived journal that you, Langston Hughes, and Wallace Thurman founded in 1925, openly casts the three of you as a protest group, and *Fire* a vehicle for an *authentic* Black literature.

Because language is central to culture and culture to identity, must Hurstonian literature be deemed counter-hegemonic? The language of *Gourd Vine, Moses,* and *Their Eyes,* is a language that seems to me to create a literary "space" for Blackness; an affirmation, or circle designed for cultural subjectivity. It is womb-like; a space in which Blacks name themselves, their temporal and spatial experiences. I always think of them, of these "folk;" their language . . . as a language of liberation. You received pressure to create non-Black characters and characters whose language is mainstream, so, some argue that your response is *Seraph on the Suwanee*. It seems that you were pulled away from your center by the forces of social criticism. What I am saying is this: If one uses general standards of measure and critical judgment that typically determine a writer's style and subject, then, until *Seraph*, you were unique. For although you were college educated, your natal community insisted on a certain level of cultural integrity by refusing to accept the "New Zora" who first attempted to collect and to record their stories.

That your natal community was unwilling to accept a "fabricated" Zora Hurston, in fact, rejected her, is much to their credit. For them you remained "family," college notwithstanding. The lesson here is one in which meaning extends beyond language to philosophy, to thought and action, all of which language implies. While your endorsement of "new words" in *Their Eyes* is well founded, your natal community refused to accept a stylized Zora who attempted to impress them with academic pretentiousness and double-talk. They responded by refusing to cooperate with your research agenda which was to collect tales. In other words, they insisted that you come to them in the form of "communicant," "family," not as "Other." Refusal to accept the "alien," was a strong indication of collective communal resistance to external agency, to domination and control. Your intent was, of course, to heighten communal pride, which suggests to some extent, that you had come to *authenticate* the *authentic*. In other words, the Eatonville community forced you to be yourself.

A current then runs through the corpus of your work that represents a philosophical worldview linked by you to the speech and language of the Black rural South. It is the authenticating language of a Black community. Those who speak the language are *insiders*, those without this language, *outsiders*. Rightly, this communal value is a literary situatedness and cultural lens that emanates from *within* community. Hence, neither you nor many other Black women fiction writers draw characters who are not located in a communal environment. I view this structural element as the most profound aspect of Black women's literary expression. Such a posture is revolutionary because it validates and rehistoricizes cultural experience placing it at the center of the individual's identity.

Thus Black women writers sustain *tradition* at two levels. First, there is *tradition* in the cultural sense of reconceptualizing a certain view of reality that resonates with experience. Second, there are contextual communal behaviors evidenced and attitudes that are consonant with a specific worldview. These writers are aware of the importance of such a synthesis in their work and its connection to the larger project of literary validation. Collectively we acknowledge the primacy of efforts to merge the past with the present and of drawing correspondences between our real and imaginative experiences. The fictional images of Black women create, revise, and correct misrepresentations of our lives.

Once again I want to look at *Gourd Vine* to illustrate the use of women as exemplars for other women and to revisit your heroine, Lucy Potts Pearson. Towards the novel's end, Lucy recognizes that death is imminent and calls her daughter, Isis, to her bedside. At that time Lucy bequeaths her feather bed to Isis—a bed purchased by Lucy with money she earned in return for seamstress work performed for a White woman. This passage is deeply symbolic. Isis is recipient of a material representation of her mother's foundational role in her life. By extension, the passage infers that Isis will build upon her mother's foundation. The reader might then envision generations of Black women who share community and build upon the accomplishments of their mothers and foremothers. *Gourd Vine*, then, illustrates generational or *vertical* images of Black women passing on a legacy—a foundation—envisioning even greater accomplishments among new generations; standing on one's ancestors' shoulders. Alternatively, *Their Eyes* provokes a *horizontal* view of the use of language among generations of Black women in community through Janie, the "storyteller"/Goddess, who transforms the consciousness of her consort and friend, Pheoby, through the use of "word magic." Incidentally, recall that in Egyptian mythology, Isis re/members the scattered parts of the body of Osiris, and makes him w*hole*.

Feel the spray of my words . . .
the sound of my voice.

The Gourd Dipper

Zora reflected on the memory of her mother lying on her death-bed, depending on what was then a very young girl for a voice. The child searched for the language that might stop her father and the other adults gathered around the dying woman from following a tradition that mandated removal of the pillow from beneath her mother's head. Another part of the tradition required that all mirrors in the room of the dying be covered. Her mother had earlier announced to her young daughter that she wanted neither tradition followed at the time of her death. Unable to muster a voice with which she might enforce her dying mother's wishes, she was aware of how deadly and guilt provoking silence can render those who are bound by it. She had thoughts and feelings about the impact and the import that her literary voice and language might have in shaping Black women's writing. Indeed, for many years she thought deeply about what might have happened to her work and her words, where they might be scattered. She never experienced a feeling of failure so long as she was working. She thought that most of her work was lost somewhere, and might never be found. But she realized that that was nearly impossible because of the way that life comes full circle. Paradoxical. Uncanny. But life is that way. The way that she reacted to her own fiction was to ask herself whether a piece would appeal to her, were she not the author. The appeal most often was there. She wondered why so few were interested. At best, public interest fluctuated. Some were at odds with her thoughts about the value of a particular novel or collection of lore or tales. When it happened, when the new wave of interest struck in the 1970s, she was stunned. But then it makes sense that she might become a part of a growing female sensibility through renderings of real and imagined characters sketched decades before this most recent women's movement.

Women are often accused of limiting themselves to writing about love relations, having little interest in, even ignoring who and what they are in other contexts. But this notion of limitation is an inaccurate assessment of women who write fiction, whether or not they center images around "romantic love." Zora believed that women writers give readers far more than tales of lovers. In *Their Eyes*, for instance, she used intimacy—love, as a background to show the nature of life within a Black southern community at a particular point in time; to illustrate a Black woman's search for wholeness, and most importantly, to make a statement about women's power to alter their lives, and influence the lives of other women. In her view *Their Eyes* accomplished these aims. Moreover, the South is the cradle of experience for Blacks in the New World, and she views everything cultural as radiating outward from that regional hearth. Of course, this belief was sometimes viewed with hostility—thought to be counter to the projected image of the "New Negro." But it seemed obvious to her that any element extracted from the source without sufficient attention to that source would result in an unfinished product. For instance, if one simply looks at an intimate relationship and fails to consider the cultural influences brought to bear on it, the inferences and outcomes of such a view would lack critical elements. For each of us, even within the same racial identity, has both a familial and a communal culture. Ignoring these factors would obscure knowledge of the path along which culture has a major impact on human behavior. More important, and even more confounding than the objection of some middle-class Blacks to the use of southern language and speech, was the fact that a majority of Blacks in northern urban areas were themselves products of southern familial roots and tradition. A direct association exists between language and identity, one which she thought important to a politics of Black aesthetics.

When she arrived in the North in the early 1920s, she noted that the sophisticated manner of the few financially secure Blacks most often bore the mark of Black southern culture. When the opportunity was presented to collect folklore in the South she seized the moment, wanting to collect folktales, and document the richness, beauty, pain, and passion of the Black experience in a southern community. The uniqueness of this lore is linked to the way that language is linked to community, identity, and history. Language it seems has a life of its own. She was anxious to offer Blacks a reflection of themselves; a mirror, so that they might see themselves, appreciate, and value their own image. Viewing the larger Black experience without the rural southern genesis, one might be led to believe that somehow or other Blacks simply "happened" to the world, from out of nowhere. Since the Great Migration from the South, Blacks have been thought to be an "urban problem." Internalized, such a view erodes one's self-esteem, and denies a collective history. Human beings, it appears, have a need to know what happened to them before their current situation; to place experience in social and political contexts. Language, the vehicle of stories, provides that link with the past. Words are essential transmitters of human identity through time and space. Words are invaluable, indispensable things. She is sure that this is true even in contemporary society. Furthermore, one fares much better when expounding on a subject that one knows well. Black life in the South, in Florida, is a subject that she knows very well. And so is love; based on personal encounter. Love and intimacy are now, and always will be, a challenge to those who dare to tread. This is so in both life and literature; literature always being a kind of reflection of life.

Women do write about love. They do so, in part, because of their attraction to the mysteries of life, and their embodiment of mystery: their menses synchronize with the phases of the moon; they produce new life, and have the necessary physiology to sustain that life in the form of breast milk. Women are personifications of mystery. So not for a lack of versatility do women write about love, but rather they write "love stories" in their search for words to clarify deep and confounding emotion. She decided to emphasize Black life, and sometimes love, within the domain of creative writing.

She was drawn to creative writing because of the latitude it allows for various forms of expression. The parameters of creativity are without existence. During periods of field work, collecting lore, the mode used for expressing her engagement with other cultures might have been as effectively "literary" as writing novels. Just a different form. This is especially true of her material on Haiti. She often felt uncertain, however, of what to do about presentation of information; how to best represent the experience and the people. At times it was quite difficult for her to continue waging a battle against more acceptable presentational forms than her own. *Tell My Horse* is, nonetheless, formatted in an unusual way as a field experience for that time. One might also think of *Mules and Men* as a counter-structure; or, a different way of writing ethnography. In *Mules* she records the words of her subjects, but, uncharacteristic of the time and the field, includes her voice, and her subjective thought, in the final research product.

To the contrary, in the midst of the passion Zora felt writing *Their Eyes*, the pencil was a balm for her seared emotion. As you might have guessed, the wide range of emotion depicted in the novel reflects the end of a personal love affair. The negative thoughts expressed in the book that Blacks hold toward one another, around issues of color and class, are also based on experience and history. Writing on these and similar topics created tension for her and sometimes strained her relations with other Black writers.

Their Eyes is not intended to be a historical work, but she believed that the linguistic confluence should be highlighted—the connection between Africa and Blacks in the West. This statement is also a reference to the belief held by many Africans in enslaved communities in the West, that their souls would return to their ancestral homeland after death. An old "Negro Spiritual" exclaims, "Ah got a home ovah yonder . . ." referring to the other side of the Atlantic, Africa, to which the slave would someday return. Many of Zora's youthful experiences bore the markings of an African past, such as the emphasis placed on orality in her community, and the African genesis of the lore and trickster tales that she so often heard: "High John the Conqueror," and "Anansi, the Spider," are examples.

She attempted to convince others of the validity of her position, without actually arguing the point, by presenting information and commentary in her narratives. The critical establishment adamantly opposed linkages between African peoples believing that Blacks would best serve in the role of objects of scientific inquiry, and servants in White households. Zora wrote against that notion by engaging a language system of southern Black language and speech—a particular way of "speaking" and "seeing" that many of her critics wished to forget, or denied ever existed.

Let me not leave you with the impression that she is more deserving of a place in the history of Black women's literary productions than are her predecessors. . . . Yes, others, many others preceded her, created a space for her, and she carried on the legacy. These were Black women! Neither should she necessarily stand out for praise because she sometimes focused attention on the African origins of certain aspects of Black life. She is adamant on this point: many of her predecessors should be remembered and honored, and some reevaluated—reconsidered in the face of the muting forces that impinged upon their lives, and their writing. A case in point is the early poet, Phillis Wheatley, who has been treated harshly by some critics. Writers write only what they can imagine. As a community of writers, Black women tend to engage issues related to or reflective of personal relationships and challenges, whether as primary theme or subtext, in novels and short stories. They write their aspirations, and experiences; speak of conflicts and trials, in real and imaginary communities. Their literarture, she believes, balances the observable tendency, in myth and folklore, to depict Black women as quasi-witches who have a fondness for deception and destruction.

Early Black women writers used various forms to express themselves in an oppressive society. The first novel written by a Black woman, Harriet E. Wilson, was titled *Our Nig, or Sketches from the Life of a Free Black*. Wilson's work was registered in 1859 for copyright. Interestingly, the publication's "Introduction" calls it "a novel, a fictional third-person autobiography." No doubt this is one of the earliest recorded "experimental" novelistic forms. We know then that early Black women writers exercised what one might call "non-canonical, unconventional narrative strategies," from the inception of our literary history. *Our Nig* reflects the author's feelings about, and experiences with, issues of race, class, and poverty. Wilson was appropriately concerned about the issue of acceptance, and wrote, "I sincerely appeal to my colored brethren universally for patronage, hoping that they will not condemn this attempt of their sister to be erudite, but rally around me a faithful bond of supporters and defenders."

This statement shows the writer's skepticism about the type of reception she might receive for having touched upon the delicate subject of racial oppression, and other acts of social injustice that she experienced and records in her work?

Lucy Terry inaguated the history of Black women as published poets with her poem *Bar's Fight* which, although written in 1746, did not come to print until 1895. Phillis Wheatley's *Poems and*

Various Subjects, published in England (1773), was the first book of poetry published by a Black American. Charlotte Forten meticulously maintained personal journals that were later published. Forten's journals were kept between 1854–1864; and 1885–1889. In 1865 Alice Nelson-Dunbar authored *Violets and Other Tales.* The turn of the century saw publication of Pauline Hopkins's novel, *Contending Forces: A Romance Illustrious of Negro Life North and South.* It is obvious that Zora Hurston walked along a path earlier tread by many others. Among her peers, in 1924, Jesse Redmon Fauset gave to the world an engaging novel, *There is Confusion.* Faucet's was the first nationally recognized novel written by a Black woman. Nella Larsen's 1928 publication, *Quicksand* was also highly acclaimed. Her *Passing,* though less well received by the critical community, proved her to be a talented writer. In the 1920s Zora had not yet written a full-length novel. At that point, she had published a few stories in the journal, *Stylus,* but had written only short fiction, such as "John Redding Goes to Sea" (1921), and "O Night," in the same year. Her first full-length work would be published a decade later than Fauset's. In the light of her predecessors' work, she contends that the tradition of Black women's writing includes a range of themes, stylistic approaches, and political postures. Most important, Black women writers acknowledge their creative work as a legitimate mode of self-expression—a venue for racial and ethnic identity and for the exploration of gender and class issues. Although they often write of "love," they are not limited in their literary focus. Larsen's *Quicksand* concerned itself with problems related to miscegenation in the lives of two Black women. Her *Passing* explores the ambiguity experienced by two Blacks who attempt to cross the color line.

The writers of whom she speaks, and many others, advanced a tradition—a tradition that explores many facets of Black life. She suggested that her politics sometimes ran counter to the views of some of the writers mentioned, especially concerning the race issue. Yet, she hastened to remind you that writers must be viewed in the milieu of the political climate of their own era. She was uncertain that she identified her work in the way that you appear to conceptualize it—that is, as "validation of a Black Self." In her youth, in Eatonville, her community simply lived across the day-to-dayness of existence. As some critics suggest, her fiction . . .

or, her "fictions," were often thinly veiled representations of certain childhood and adult experiences. Very early childhood images.

When Zora contemplated the "child/woman," she found the word combination interesting, in the sense that you explore passages from her autobiography in which she recalls her mother's death. In that time of crisis that was her mother's impending death she, the child, was expected to assume a woman's voice. The entire scene remained relivable and the feelings associated with the experience easily recalled. The remembrance of her mother gazing up at her, expecting something, expecting something that a young girl of nine years could not provide. Zora wrote about her sense of failure in *Dust Tracks*. As a nine-year-old, she could not force her own will against the collective will of the elders in her mother's room. Least of all, could she have rebuked her father. She sensed her own helplessness, and felt a deep sense of failure—tragic failure in her mother's final hour. Suffering, and self-blame haunted her for many years to come. In *Dust Tracks* she attempts to expose the pain that was for so long hers: She "wrote" the pain, hoping to explain, and erase it from her heart:

> I was to agonize over that moment for years to come. In the midst of play, in wakeful moments after midnight, on the way home from parties, and even in the classroom during lectures. My thoughts would escape occasionally from their confines and stare me down. Now I know that I could not have had my way against the world. The world we lived in required those acts. Anything else would have been sacrilege, and no nine-year-old voice was going to thwart them. My father was with the mores. He had restrained me physically from outraging the ceremonies established for the dying. If there is any consciousness after death, I hope that Mama knows that I did my best. She must know how I have suffered for my failure. (617–18)

One way that she thought might make up for her failure, the inability to follow her mother's deathbed wishes, was to later exercise her own woman-voice, powerfully and vehemently, to express her beliefs and opinions in the interest of women and children. Her mother's gaze, and her words often seared through Zora like liquid fire. She began to, consciously, speak for her mother, for herself, and for other women who were victims and subjects of silence. Coming to use her voice on her own, for herself and for others, was an expression of her deepening self-

confidence, and enlarging empathy for those without the privilege of voice. The issue of voice, and privilege, carried over or
was reflected in the subjects emphasized in her writing. The rich,
the elite, and bourgeoise worlds drowned out the voices of poor,
Black, and ordinary women. She was thought by some to be a
"carefree spirit," but that label was a reference to the voice, her
voice, often heard in those spaces typically reserved for Whites
and men. More than "carefree," she realized then that her attitude toward speech, and speaking out were politically dangerous. The greatest danger lay in her financial lack. She was vulner-
able simply by not having the wherewithal to meet financial
obligations. Despite that reality, she was not emotionally fragile
because she had lived on the edge for so long. It was hard to
keep the two realities separate: the objective reality of her dependence on others for financial sustenance and the subjective
view of herself as an unencumbered woman of strong voice and
committed opinion. Dependence of any kind had always been a
psychological burden. These facts, nothwithstanding, patron support was barely sufficient to make ends meet. Rarely, even at the
peak of her writing productivity, were there very many of those
extras most of us savor. She was trapped between the old "devil
and deep, blue sea," "damned if she did, and damned if she
didn't." She was without a way out, you see? The never-ending
poverty, and parallel dependence created emotional tension and
forced compromises that she would rather not have made. A
compromise: The requirement to submit manuscripts to benefactors for review, and critique sometimes caused her to write
tentatively.

Her financial vulnerability stirrred thoughts about this America,
your America, and your "Democracy." America is . . . well, it's
very interesting, and so is that thing called "Democracy." Your
democracy works strange tricks on the psyche. Most feel that in
a democratic society certain rights and freedoms are guaranteed—
guaranteed for everyone. She is not thinking, now, of the freedom to vote or even whether, say, Blacks are free to ride buses
with Whites. Not that kind of freedom. When one gets right down
to the matter, the kind of freedom that she pondered had to do
with the nature of her personal experiences as a Black woman,
an ethnographer, folklorist, and novelist. For many years she felt
sure that persistence was a virtue, and if she continued to move

as though she were part of a "real democracy," with, say, privilege of voice, she might sell the ideas that were central to her creative work. These ideas included order, intelligence, integrity, and the capacity for human caring—human characteristics identifiable among most cultures. She was wrong. "Democracy," and "freedom" were not to be taken seriously, not in real life. She learned that America did not intend the idea to be taken seriously by Blacks. You will recall the essay that she wrote on the subject in 1945, "Crazy for This Democracy." Polemical? Ah, Yes! Her work was misunderstood by some, and deprecated by others—Blacks unable to see, for example, the race consciousness and concern . . . the connection between the fictional and the real.

Ms. Turner, a character in *Their Eyes* is a composite sketch of several forms of race consciousness prevalent among Blacks in the America of the 1930s. Ms. Turner's view of herself is that she is superior to other Blacks because of her lighter skin, straighter hair, and the angularity of her nose than, say, Tea Cake. Ms. Turner is profoundly disdainful towards Tea Cake, a result of his dark skin and African features. How can Janie (a mulatto) bear such ugliness? Ms. Turner abhors her own social place, and Whites will not create a special one for her, fair skin notwithstanding. She desires a separate category from that of blacker Blacks. A true mark of . . . the stain of self-disdain. The critique of blackness that Ms. Turner represents runs counter to the existence of true Democracy; it renounces the intrinsic social equality that democracy demands. More pointedly, what passes for democracy is an abstraction of the real thing, for this unreal thing masks a full compliment of ubiquitous wrongs against the unempowered, whether they represent race, gender or social class issues. Those who have extracted power for themselves share a deep interest in, and a commitment to, maintaining the mirage. Ms. Turners's point-of-view is "learned," and sustained by existing social forces and powerful individuals, and groups, within the society. Unfortunately, it appears that those who have not yet empowered themselves will continue to suffer. The Ms. Turners of the world aspire to emulate the most anti-humane characteristics of the empowered. As Zora wrote, elsewhere, democracy is an ideal state that should be vigorously pursued by all. Capturing the essence of democracy appears as difficult as catching the tail-end of a dream.

The powerful who know the truth are often working to forget the downtrodden and become deeply enmeshed in maintaining the prevailing attitudes and behaviors of control.

There is also a Black and female politics in America. Both of these categories—"Black" and "female" (are categories marked by social constraint. Ms. Turner is prototypical of one aspect of this politics: the politics of color. The other side of the coin, the concern for gender is a double yoke worn by women of color. Zora knows that detractors closely scrutinize every move made by a Black woman who gains a modicum of recognition or success, her "burden" notwithstanding. What they actually measure is how far from the historical stereotype of Black womanhood she strays. She will likely receive less criticism the closer her physical type to the characteristics so loved and demanded by the Ms. Turners of the world. An explanation might go this way: Western culture retains a vision of Black women as "nannies," and "pickaninnies," not writers, college presidents, magistrates, and scientists. These images—"nanny" and "pickaninny"—are still on the eyeball of the country and challenge every Black woman, every day of her life, in both subtle and overt ways. For Black women, ourselves, this is a remnant image of our historical debasement; baggage carried over from slavery in the West. Sadly, she says (and, surely, you know), we have learned even to use these images against one another. To be thought of, imagined only in this way—hypersexualized beings and producers of a free labor force, is to deny our humanity. Many, many Black women have challenged the odds and strive to reverse these conditions. Ms. Turner's blindness, her incredulity at the thought of Janie's love for the black-skinned Tea Cake, is overshadowed only by her ill-begotten admiration for Janie's mulatto features. How might a "Democracy" create a Ms. Turner? Her self-disdain for blackness denies democracy's existence in any true sense.

Obviously, Janie ventures outside the realm of her socially prescribed space of "light-skinness." In fact, she mocks her placement there, and shows a keen desire for blackness—Tea Cake's blackness. Their romance is associated with her search for wholeness. His blackness balances that part of her "Self" that was shriveled by two generations of rape, acts of degeneracy that created the mulatto. Ms. Turner is confounded—needs a crystal ball, an oracle, to make sense of Janie's innermost desire for such a man.

Her own desire for the evaporation of the Tea Cakes of the world is singularly blinding. Never has the thought occurred to Ms. Turner that Janie's motives are self-expression and love.

You see, literature offers a field for the expression of our political consciousness, and writing as political action is a fertile venue. Revolution you know begins in the mind; and can, therefore, reside in literary spaces. To think and write outside the social norm is a revolution of the mind; the primary site for change in society. Ms. Turner . . . poor Ms. Turner was the victim of her own desperation and denial?

There is so much that Zora wishes to say about the politics of a woman's writing, about the magic in women's words, and the politics that those words portend. Writing is a response to and a translation of the social space of a woman's psyche, if not always her actual existence. Most often it is held up against her movement in the social world. If, for example, as a writer, she violates social expectations of women, she is less threatening than the woman writer whose life and literature extend the boundaries of her social, and political space. The world, you see, remains somewhat shocked by the broken silence of a woman outside the domestic realm. And the mindfields that mark her path are many; the care she must exercise as she walks is great. For such a woman, the one who speaks and acts in the public sphere, may be viewed as a traitor; a debunker of myths, and a comfort-zone breaker. She is like a voice that has come back from the dead. What she struggled to say here is, perhaps, more than may be stated by the use of words.

The Black woman begins her life journey on the edge, on the periphery; she enters the world in the margin. She speaks and writes from within a circle of female and male associates who are also struggling to be heard as much by their cultural kin as by the majority, or mainstream. Both groups are likely to shrink from her if she is strongly opinionated and self-affirming. Few will understand. She will suffer the punishment of social isolation and alienation for transgressing the social order. And, of course, once committed to a position in writing, there is small chance of her ever modifying the printed word, even as she grows and changes— learns herself, and acquires greater knowledge and better understands the politics of gender. The result is that the political identity attributed to a woman who writes is, generally, linked to her first (perhaps, her only) publication. Women, too, have the potential for change, she says, happily! The other side of this female conundrum is related to opportunity. For writing requires time, a commodity that is sorely lacking in the lives of many women, for women often lead double, and triple lives, you know: mother, wife, homemaker. . . . Readers too often have a single snapshot of a woman's beliefs, and they hold tightly to that image. Ideally, there would be space, time, and support for a single writer to produce multiple works. She was fortunate to have the will, freedom, and fortitude to present different perceptions of her worldview, and to show herself in evolution. Although even her evolved opinions were not necessarily popular.

She noted earlier that many women remain silent throughout their lives, with great stories, wisdom, and truths fomenting in their souls and psyches. No doubt a significant number of them fear social wrath, isolation, and predictable cruelty. Fortunately, from what she is able to make of it, Black women, young and old, increasingly accept the risk, step out, and assume a posture of confidence, if not fearlessness. They write their stories in their own way, according to the world of their experience. A prime motive of intimidation, of silencing, is to cause the uninitiated woman writer such fear and trembling that she retreats into darkness, into silence and obscurity. The poetics of her life and her world never escape contemplation, and imprisonment. (Thoughts sometimes scatter . . . fly away—I chase and catch them again).

Zora understood that several social scientists who claimed to have studied the Black community in the twentieth century fixed their gaze on the Black woman, and they concluded that she exhibits erratic, aberrant behavior. You recall, the "black matriarchy"-type study. Some "scientists" even suggest that it is the Black mother who often causes her children's poor academic performance and failure to achieve. These accounts demonize Black women without even superficial attention to the social forces that she must confront. They attempt to show the difference between the focus of Black women's novels about love, mothering, motherhood, and community—all political topics—and the essence of "scientific studies." No attempt is made to take into account the challenges Black women face raising children in a racialized society. Harrassment is a factor in the lives of Black females, but it is a fact of disgraceful reality for the young Black man-child.

Black women's fiction and poetry tell who and what they are, unveiling values, desires, challenges, and much more. The Black woman's true identity escapes scientific research because of the way "science" is practiced, often with built-in biases. Matriarchy? The term "matriarchy" is inappropriately descriptive of our life roles. Might a Black matriarchy exist if Black women are the poorest, single group in society—Black women and their children? An inference of power and authority resides in the notion of matriarchy. We are not in Africa you know, and the term has been scandalized here. The problem stems from the dominant culture's view of Black life as, essentially, pathological and pathetic. The term matriarchy, associated with African social systems is superimposed on Africa's New World descendants and given meaning drawn out of science rather than taken from Black culture and tradition. In "science" negative connotation replaces social order and the generative energy, which is the primacy of those meanings that are a part of African tradition. Fictions by Black women stand as correctives to the misinterpretation of history made expedient by modern science. "Science," you see, requires an accounting of all phenomena, even for the unmeasurable. The problems of science for Black women become representation, wrongly historicizing Black women's experience. One outcome of such misrepresentation is that the Black woman remains a Venus Hottentot. A bizzare curiosity. A Black female curiosity is labeled "deviant," "sinister," "witch," and "mad."

As early as the late nineteenth century, Black women writers attempted to "tell their story," to speak their yearnings, and articulate the agony of voicelessness. Anna Julia Cooper is especially important for her 1892 non-fictional work, *A Voice From the South.* In that work Cooper speaks directly to Black women's sensibility. In Cooper, and in others, we see tradition in the making, a tradition in its infancy. Think about it. When those who are called deficient continue to speak, to seek power and authority in the face of the war chants of their enemies; when they raise their voices confident and strong, are not their voices even greater proof of their strangeness? Oddly, Black women writers provide grist for the naysayers' mill. They write and write whatever the cost. Witches. Bewitching Witches. Witches with stories to tell. Cats with nine lives.

The politics of Black femaleness is a decidedly complex politics; tricky business. Its complexity is related to a historical conspiracy against truthfulness and accuracy in depictions of Black women by others, the medium, notwithstanding. Black women are seldom shown in healthy relationships with their men, with other women, their children, and certainly not with history. These relationships form the architecture of our psyches that have been framed over hundreds of years since the beginning of Black time in captivity. Zora thought she would remind you that the dominant literature of a society tends to represent and reinforce the moral and social assertions of a particular historical attitude or vision, one that may not necessarily be in agreement with the historical subject's reality and experience. Does this mean that all human history is inaccurate if not written by the subject? She would say, at best, that such history is skewed by perspectives of time and political interest. Yet experience is not the single legitimate interpretive apparatus. But insight comes from drawing one's conclusions from the vantage point of those whose lives such events have touched.

A sensitive reading and deep understanding of the thoughts and lives of early Black women writers has great value for the present social position that Black women hold. When one considers that the first published works by Blacks in America were written by women, perhaps the term, "matriarchy," enters the minds of some, no matter how inappropriate. The obstructionists (they come in many forms) persist in drawing antiquated conclusions and will resist reasoned analysis and self-articulated definitions of Black womanhood. These early literatures obviously defy historical and contemporary Black female prototypes, especially those prevalent in the West, since the late nineteenth, and early twentieth centuries. Progenitors of early Black literatures were very likely moved by both a sense of responsibility and the need for self-expression—the ability to interpret and write their lives and the lives of their communities. She is adamant on this point. This is so because creative literature, and non-fiction prose are didactic instruments of social and political change among literate, oppressed masses the world over. The self-initiated printed word (along with political activism, dance, and other art forms) influences minds and challenges received notions of "otherness."

Let's go back now to Zora's early researches, and an important point can be made here. When she first traveled home, to Eatonville, on a folklore collecting trip, she was considered an outsider among the people there. The problem was one that she created, a problem of language usage and attitude. Approaching her Floridian friends from the angle of scholar was simply an affront. They rejected her, thought her to be pretentious, and haughty. There she was "the scholar" who would dare not "speak the language of the folk." She was summarily dismissed! At most, she would only collect very basic material. There would be none of the inside stories, the *real* ones, until she shifted her attitude, and convinced the storytellers of the *value* that she placed on their values, and what they had to say, by shifting away from language that ran counter to their culture, identity, and tradition. She later showed them that she was still the Zora they knew. She altered her use of language and pattern of speech to match theirs. That shift was proof of her legitimacy and community membership. You see, she had really wanted to show them that she had studied anthropology, and was learned, so they might be proud of one of their own making it in the North, in the big city. Contrarily, communities tend to resent one of their own who separates from them and returns obviously "different" and affected. Her "performance" was dropped as a result of their lack of acceptance of it. Her error in perception corrected, the home community offered an outpouring of stories and tales. She learned, too, the importance of her participation in the "performance" of their storytelling. Small-town people tend to hide their secrets and time-honored tales from outsiders and from insiders who, in some manner, estrange themselves from the community. Among these Floridians, storytelling, reciting their lore, is ritualized. Appropriately, she refers to their storytelling or "lying sessions" as ceremony, and a reinscription of group identity through words "enacted" in a particular manner, in a certain space and time.

Communal ritual and protocol exist in all culturally and socially organized groups around the world. It's sort of this way: when particular actions and behaviors are viewed as bearing power over the group's destiny and identity, these activities become ritualized and protected. Her friends in Eatonville demonstrated a lesson that she understood, only theoretically, from textbooks.

Despite early problems related to the way that she represented herself at home, she believed that she understood, more profoundly, what was expected of her, and adjusted quickly to other such situations in southern groups and communities. This is not to suggest that all was well in each subsequent collecting attempt, but the lesson was a handy one. Her southern background notwithstanding, she was, admittedly, sometimes both threatened by and threatening to others in those settings. Moving within many rural southern communities, she was grateful for her southern background because, on occasion, her safety and well-being depended on her knowledge of southern, regional habits. She later laughed about having gone home on that lore collecting trip, speaking like a student in a college classroom. Now that was performance; the high-flying language and all!

She could not, honestly, deny that education had affected her. The life that she believed to be deliciously ordinary, her life in Eatonville, she had learned was a "collectible." Yes, maybe she was different. But her love for the lore of her youth and her respect for the people who performed it were unchanged. Yes, and maybe they viewed her differently, too. In a sense, she was torn by two sets of views of who and what she should be: too southern in the North; too northern in the South. Well, she decided just to be herself . . . Black, female, and southern. Afterwards . . . after the incident, she thought it interesting that she could be "natural" in the presence of northern Whites but had felt a need to impress southern Blacks. Back home they wanted to see the same old Zora that they remembered before her college experience and the North. The real lesson was that she learned to be herself . . . just to be herself.

Conversely, her southern background contributed, she believed, to the skewed view some held of her and these beliefs added to her marginal status among particular writers in New York. Not only was she the rare female in the Harlem setting, but she was also a product of a very different cultural experience from most of her associates—the product of an all-Black, southern town. She was "different" from the men who were at the center of the New Negro movement of the 1920s and 1930s. Her manner and style were thought obtuse by some; "country" by others. Her speech reflected her southern roots. She enjoyed cooking, and dining on southern cuisine. Further, she was known to

"perform" storytelling sessions at parties, much like those that
were so much a part of her youth.

Because of the way that she presented herself, there was little
doubt about her southern background—a decidedly different one
from most of her colleagues. Though the majority Black population of any major northern city is simply a human artery branched
off from its southern source, among the New Negro elite of the
period, Zora personified regional difference. There were those
associates in New York, and in other northern cities, who were
very self-consciously attempting to rid themselves of any obvious vestige of southern tradition, particularly, within the realms
of their public and professional lives. Few of her peers, themselves, grew up in the South. The last impression an authentic
"New Negro" would want to leave was that of southern heritage,
or personal familiarity with rural, southern folk tradition. So the
politics of living Black and female was complicated by a regional
bias. In essence, this was an issue related to a perception of class.
After all, would some "New Negroes" announce their race were
it not for the obvious?

Nevertheless, among some few of the Black "literati," there
were men who relished southern cuisine and made themselves
available for rent parties and the cabarets that Blacks could frequent. "Undignified" music and behavior out of alignment with
the majority population were thought to be an impediment to
the elevation of the race. What she meant is that some of her
contemporaries strove to behave more White-like than the Whites
who flocked to the clubs and cabarets to be entertained by Blacks
whose performance was often simply a public revue based on
Black "street talk" and dance. Zora thought little of whether she
was supposed to act "colored." "She simply was!" "Do I love
myself?" she asked. If so, then that love necessarily extended to
and included her background. True, she was nearly always financially strapped, but that had noting to do with race and regional
pride. Neither her southern roots nor her race was a tragedy.

In the North, in Harlem, there were accusations of Zora "cut-
ting the fool" for Whites. Without oversimplifying things, she was
simply being herself. Zora. Why smother a part of her personality, especially the part that celebrated her cultural uniqueness?
What actually happened, she believes, is that Whites felt comfortable and "entertained" by her southernness, because

southernness was thought to be "raw" and "uninhibited." There were all of those "pictures in the heads" of Whites about the bizarre ways of the formerly enslaved, particularly enslaved women, and these images persisted. These beliefs were held by many of the downtown Whites who came uptown to cabarets on weekends for a brief sojourn into the world of Black, excotica.

A benefactor, Charlotte Osgood Mason, in fact, *insisted* that Zora write the colorful, entertaining aspects of southern folk-culture into her work. It was not that Zora disagreed, in substance, but rather that she objected in principle to her patron's insistence on control of the writing as Zora's primary financial resouce. She resented, too, the insinuation that there was something "antediluvian" or "primitive" about people who used language in a certain way. Osgood Mason's control motive evoked her dismay and consternation. Zora consistently felt the greatest and most persistent discomfort around representations of Black life and culture in fiction, and White patrons' fixed views about Black life. During the 1920s and 1930s they typically insisted that their "perspective" show through in their proteges' writing. And she spoke out about the considerable level of control that Charlotte Osgood Mason exercised over her life and work. The fact is that patrons strongly influenced the nature of the Harlem writers' work, and, to some considerable extent, that influence was psychologically vexing. She aimed to recognize the people that she wrote about on their terms and in their cultural contexts. She did not wish to depict them as artifacts or curiosities. There are critics who have suggested that her work depended on arcane subject matter: rural Black life. To a certain extent, this allegation is correct, she agrees. Her finest works celebrate Black, rural, southern, traditional culture. As many writers do, she wrote best about her deepest interest; she followed the path of creative energy that led to Eatonville. For her this path was also one of evolution, and self-revelation. There was cultural richness and wisdom in the traditions of her small-town people, and she wanted to record their wisdom before the townsfolk stopped telling the stories; urgent anthropology was her project. For Zora these tales were valued, not curiosities. *In Mules and Men*, she comments on the impact the tradition of storytelling had on her thinking. She wrote:

> I thought about the tales I had heard as a child. How even the Bible was made over to suit our vivid imagination. How the devil always outsmarted

God and how that over-noble hero Jack or John—not *John Henry*, who occupies the same place in Negro folk-lore that Casey Jones does in white lore and if anything is more recent—outsmarted the devil. Brer Fox, Brer Deer, Brer 'Gator, Brer Dawg, Brer Rabbit, Ole Massa and his wife were walking the earth like natural men way back in the days when God himself was on the ground and men could talk with him. Way back there before God weighed up the dirt to make the mountains. . . . (10, 11)

Perhaps because of the vast reservoir of stories and tales she recalled, there was little need to invent or create themes, drawn from a less interesting universe. She had in the folk, vivid, real images, characters, and situational frames of reference born of memory and experience. Memory was the most potent reservoir from which to draw novelistic characters. She used memory to evoke cultural context. The fictional characters that she presented were out-of-life, and "authentic." Authenticity was also the impetus for developing the "radical" journal, *Fire*, with one-time close friend, Langston Hughes. Wallace Thurman joined them in that endeavor. The three of these Harlem writers were interested in presenting "authentic" Black literature. Still, the project was short-lived. The time was not right for them—not right for *Fire*. By "authentic," they meant Black literature in which the masses of Black people could find themselves, others, and, perhaps, their communities. Whites also sought "authenticity" in a mysterious Black ritual; a dark encounter. Some Blacks played the game; instantaneously acquiring "performance language" (when it was not there) costuming and assuming a minstrel-like posture. Most important, these performers assumed a carnivalesque version of authentic Black life. Scenarios such as this were performed in small out-of-the-way cafes, cabarets, dance halls, and brothels uptown. Harlem, in those days, was not unlike many modern tourist traps in poor countries around the world. Tourism was then, and is now, a vastly lucrative enterprise for the producers of the "exotic." Certain economies depend on such attractions. (Well . . . Brazil is one place). Many tourists take with them the cultural baggage created by desire, photo-journalism, and fantasy. They then participate in the incarnation of the exoticized population. Tourists are, typically, steered away from the day-in-the-lives of exoticized people. The people, themselves, become the artifact, the product.

The Harlem of her era was thought to be the stronghold of Black exotica and community population remnants of a lost "tribe." On any weekend Harlemites could see throngs from the more chic addresses in Manhattan flocking to dance halls, and clubs where Black women sang and shimmied. White men lusted after their fantasies and sought encounters with eroticized Black women, hoping to prove believed myths of their sexuality, "extraordinaire," seduction and seditiousness. Her one-time friend, Carl Van Vechten, was considered by many (uptown Blacks, and downtown Whites) to be "Chief Guide and Tour Master" of the nightlife scene uptown. Van Vechten's *Nigger Heaven* (1926) was an attempt to capture the quality of Harlem night life and culture during that era. The book engages much of the language and phraseology known to have attracted White thrill-seekers and suggests, if not promises, a wild and memorable encounter for the daring.

Some writers who were at the center of the Harlem literary community panned the book. She was not particularly critical of it, for it contained shadows of truth about Harlem and, furthermore, harshly panning the novel seemed politically unwise. Van Vechten was the most "connected" White male known to Black writers. Zora once wrote that Van Vechten's book "revealed" Negroes of wealth and culture to the White public. *Nigger Heaven* actually created greater curiosity about Black life and aroused skepticism. It made folks "want to know." Is she admitting here that she was a political dilettante? Obviously so, to some extent. She also saw Van Vechten as an ally in those days. Friends were few and loneliness plentiful. The strongest critics of Van Vechten's work viewed it in the most negative sense: an insult to the hospitable treatment that he enjoyed among Black writers and entertainers.

Most of her New York associates were aware that she was formally educated. But that realization, that is, her formal education was another pocket of confusion. The prevailing opinion was that it was the responsibility of educated Blacks to prove that 'Negroes had culture, too.' So all of that down-home "baby" this and "sugar" that should be trashed. Often educated members of the race confront a double-edged sword. The expectation is that one must adopt "White speech, and manners" and ought to distance oneself from all tell-tale signs of the uneducated and "uncultured." Evidence of culture for her simply meant living as herself. Steeped as she was in rural southern "culture," there appeared to be no need to alter herself for different audiences. Her language, speech, and food preferences reflected a specific cultural orientation. Had she grown up in another place, at another time, she might have felt the need to redesign herself. In the environment of her youth, there was that identifiable language that expressed an internalized view of the world through a particular cultural lens. She had learned to value certain community particularities. To have denied her background or to have traded it for a remade "self," would, perhaps, have caused others to think her to be less obtruse—maybe even a "credit to her race." Perhaps Van Vechten enjoyed her company because, for him, she corroborated his feelings of "natural" superiority, or confirmed notions of his cultural dominance. Zora, the exotic?

For her it seems that formal education should place one at the center of one's cultural milieu, and open one's eyes to embrace the larger human family. In addition to helping to prepare us to live in the world with others, education should be among the more humanizing events of our lives, not the opposite. Anyway, there she was, an educated Black woman who, in the view of some, behaved as though she was an *uncultured, uneducated* Negro. Translated, that means that she loved telling jokes and stories—those tall tales that she grew up hearing in Eatonville. In that sense, the scholarships and grants that she was awarded and the money paid in tuition for her was wasted. She was aware of the anticipated change that the university was to have had and could slip into that vernacular, with all of its affectations (such as she attempted during her first collecting trip to Eatonville). But she learned her lesson and came to her senses after that first trip home. Therefore, whenever she had more than a few dollars beyond her expenses and was in the mood for company, she could be counted on to throw a party. The menu always included something "in the pot"—greens, chili, and cornbread. She consumed as much as she wanted, that is before the onset of serious stomach problems. Hers was a healthy appetite. High energy? Indeed, she had it! Zora was a woman who could write for hours during a party—or afterwards. Sometimes with a deadline to meet, and a party in full swing, she would close her mind to her surroundings, close the bedroom door and give herself over to writing words, as if alone in the world.

Fortunately, by the time she attended any of those fancy northern schools, experiences of affirmation were soundly entrenched. These feelings came at a very young age from the Eatonville community. Her pride and confidence in the viability of Black life, and expressions of Black culture were virtually unshakable by outsiders. A painful lesson that she later learned was that insiders have the opportunity to inflict greater pain than outsiders. Ultimately, Zora suffered this reality in a most devastating way.

College education had been an interesting experience. She filtered ideas through her internal categories for the attribution of meaning to world phenomena. If the facts and figures involved in a particular theory conflicted with her experience, demeaned or deprecated her identity and sensibility, she gave little credence to them. That is, she retained the main ideas, extracted the essence, and rejected the inference. The negative and the debilitating could not reach her sense of identity. Understanding the college experience as she did, that is the political nature of education, is the precise reason that she attached such importance to teaching young children about their history and culture. If this core identity is developed very early, to disrupt it would require more than life's ordinary hardships.

Had she placed herself in a position where she might be forced to behave one way with one group, and then find another "self" for others, she would have drifted into total confusion; her energy dissipated and scattered. There would have been little left to write. To the contrary, the Eatonville community had also educated her. They so convinced her—by the daily rhythm of their lives, and the power of community tradition, a part of which was orality and storytelling—that she owned a place in the world, a strong wind was required to move her. This message came in myriad ways, but the basic message assured her that she owned the right to exist in the world and to live as herself. She did have the impression that Blacks elsewhere might have had more of life's material comforts, yet her community never paid them homage. Their attention and energy was directed toward meeting the challenges of the day, and living life to the fullest, which included laughter and love, and for the men particularly, a generous portion of "honest" lying rounded out their lives.

But all of life is political. The post-Civil War political tension between the North and South is one good example. Blacks in the North, most of whom migrated after Reconstruction, and some whose forebearers were enslaved there, adopted northern attitudes toward southeners, considering the South the more backward region of the country. Politics touches all of society, and we are all opinionated, whether or not we speak our opinions. But Zora spoke out on political issues that, to her, were provocative. Her maturity brought with it more entrenched opinion, as her published essays of the 1940s illustrate. This political voice deeply complicated her life. Some already believed that she was an educated woman who behaved as though she were a country "zigaboo!" But to offer clearly political opinion was to tread on sacred, hallowed ground, for politics was surely the domain of males. If she insisted on displaying an appreciation for "rural life" in her writing, this might be tolerated, but how dare she speak out on important political issues. No doubt this was behavior well outside the domain of "Negro womanhood." Dare she to speak as a social critic? First, she was politically incorrect for the form and themes of her fiction. But to write on politics in America would bring even harsher criticism than any of her storytelling or "lack of poise." They suggested that she could not represent the feelings and thoughts of the Black population. Nevertheless, she spoke out on any political issues on her own behalf. The consensus, of course, was that comments made by any Black person represented the sentiments of the entire uncomplicated race. How alarming and almost as far-fetched as believing that Whites can speak for Blacks or men for women. She simply exercised her right to personal citizenship unabridged by membership in the Black race.

The Eatonville community had seemed quite capable of self-expression: the front porch of Joe Clarke's grocery store nothing less than a stage for storytelling and pure self-expression. Early lessons remain in our psyches, you know? She spoke as Zora Neale Hurston, not as a self-appointed spokeswoman for the race. (Anna Julia Cooper's observation about when and where the Black woman enters the social and political world comes to mind). So, although her perception was that of the individual, her voice, it seems, implicated the race. From time to time, at the apex of her life of writing, when the wrath of the keepers of Black racial integrity would fall upon her, she occasionally wondered whether they understood that her literary intent was to tell good stories— often, of real people, and to celebrate and memorialize Black culture. But she also had a research agenda. Primary on that agenda was collecting and preserving stories of a specific time and place.

Writing and reporting the old stories was a source of comfort and an impetus to reflection. When in good health, she was less conscious of the absence of enduring friendships in her life. Perhaps many writers in Harlem then never allowed themselves the opportunity to develop friendships nor allowed those they experienced to grow. With few exceptions they were short-term and sporadic. Competition for financial support from benefactors was an issue and available time scarce. Only after all of the writing, the parties, and travel—when that was nearly over (or over for her) she sensed how she longed for close relationships with other Black women. Having come from a strong, close community to one where everyone was very much left to her or his own devices for survival required a major adjustment in the early years. Friendships came hard. Deep trust was infrequent in the literary community, with few exceptions, and the trust that existed was largely between males.

These were very political times, with great uncertainty. Yes. Real questions existed among Black leaders. Opinions varied widely around which might be the surest path to Black equality. World War I had created a new political consciousness among those Black men who returned from the war only to suffer Jim Crowism at home. The attitudes of these former soldiers were ripe for bolder forms of political engagement and Black expressive art. Yet there was no clear and concise history for the collective literary philosophy that was throbbing in the hearts of Black writers and intellectuals. There was a certain awareness of history, both past and that in the making. Unreconciled groups were anxious to express what they believed to be the artistic and intellectual essence of Black life. At times the factions were in agreement. Often they were not. But the energy was there, and they moved with that energy.

Few of them were ever sufficiently solvent to write their deepest truths. The Black intelligentsia had it over the creative writers and artists because most Black intellectuals were employed and earned salaries. Some were actually heading organizations. They were free by comparison to those who looked almost exclusively to writing for their livelihood, for their survival. In a sense, one might say that the writers were held in a kind of bondage. Nearly every White socialite had a 'Pet Negro,' whom they invited to high-profile events. Zora would later write a polemical piece, "The Pet Negro System" that reflected this aspect of Black writers' lives. Artists of other mediums were also the subjects of patronage. No doubt that Blacks in America have not since that time experienced the same psychological mood as existed then, except perhaps during the 1960s. Obviously, similar motives and social focus sparked Black writers associated with New Negro movement and writer-activists who emerged during the Civil Rights Movement. Both movements centered around a concern for human dignity, and human rights. Some 'New Negro' writers hoped to convince Whites of their acumen for intellectual endeavors—their ability to create ideas and theories. These writers constituted one faction. Another faction aspired to a politics of art in the from of creative writing. Civil Rights activists of the 1960s and 1970s demanded equal education, and equality in the public sphere. In both historic periods there was a demand for equality which neither fully accomplished. Zora seems convinced that while social movements are necessary to heighten the awareness of the larger society to specific issues, finite revolution looks like Janie Mae Crawford . . .

Half Moon: "Sometimes Ah'm Up, Sometimes Ah'm Down. . . ."

I love sunshine the way it is done in Florida. Rain the same way—in great slews or not at all. I dislike cold weather and all of its kinfolk, that takes in bare trees and a birdless morning.

Zora Neale Hurston, *Dust Tracks on a Road*

Zora, in essence, I agree with your assessment of Janie Mae Crawford as a revolutionary woman—each woman must search for her freedom. But it seems to me that much more than revolution or freedom, Harlem Renaissance writers actually engaged in a search for spiritual liberation. Their collective search aimed to free the spirit or the consciousness of Blacks through a new literary aesthetic; a new awareness of forms of literary expression. In this sense, definition of the term *struggle* in the 1920s and 1930s differed, substantially, from that of the 1960s. What is clear to me, also, is there were divergent views of how to best accomplish the goal of aesthetic, and spiritual liberation among your Harlem peers. Yes, the lines were drawn between two groups: those who held a particular view of what should be the evolving Black literary aesthetic, an aesthetic that more closely resembled the prevailing White, male prose fiction and poetry model, and the group we might call the "renegades." The renegades embraced a vision of a body of literature that gave emphasis to a dramatic, yet authentic portrayal of Black folk tradition, and Black urban life. Wallace Thurman, Langston Hughes, and you were the vanguard of the renegades. Also interested in race and class issues was the Jamaican, Claude McKay. Although you may not have had leadership status within that group, you were, ideologically, the writer least like the literary establishment. Of course, arguments concerning literary form and substance among Blacks, cut across groups and, at times, approached near character assassination.

And, as one might expect, the most powerful men had the greatest influence. I wonder whether you feel that there is some benefit in looking further into what was then the general mood of the country, so that I might better understand your thoughts, say, as compared to prevailing political opinion. But most importantly, my interest centers around your life during the period between the Stock Market crash in 1929 and publication of your last novel, *Seraph on the Suwanee*, in 1948. I know that the crash of the market affected the entire country, and those of meager resources felt the brunt of that economic chaos. Yet, I am saddened by the reality that you never realized the financial fruits of your writing in a manner similar to that that individuals and publishers now gain from your publications. This picture is particularly striking in view of the level of artistic productivity you sustained between 1934 and 1939. On the other side, when taking into account the full scope of the politics involved in the production of Black literature, then as now, the level of my personal agitation is reduced. I use the word politics here in its more pejorative application. Separating the writing from the writer is a challenge most readers and critics fail to meet. We have discussed, for example, the political implications that a woman's marital status has for her professional life. We have not talked about your own marriages. The literature suggests that you were married, at least twice, between 1934 and 1939. That both of these marriages were of such short duration—neither lasting a full year—causes me to ponder your notion of what are the most critical elements of an intimate relationship. Did the brevity of these marriages turn on, or reflect, irreconcilability between your perception of a "good" relationship, and the lived experience of marriage? You tell us that one of your mates was unable to accept the primacy of work within the framework of your life together.

Also, in the early 1930s, you encountered serious health problems, even though few were aware of their full scope. You also were rather politically vocal during this period, and became the target of more criticism from your peers and others. This conflict was related to some of the beliefs and ideas that you expressed. Were these certain beliefs others held about you based on their misinterpretations of your ideas? Unless we sketch a full portrait that places you, the woman, in the flow, and stream of a social world, important inferences are sure to be missed.

Nonetheless, the mystery of Zora Neale Hurston continues, although some of the mystery is now transformed, and has become adoration for many. I have researched your life and work using all of the tools at my disposal, and, yet, there is an unknowable aspect of your life. Photographs of you, for instance, taken within the same period of time portray the "different selves" you presented to the world. Those missing pieces about your life that remain hidden from public view, and public discourses, create a mixture of mystery and adoration, and some anger. It seems to me that you had to have had a part of yourself for yourself. The you that was preserved for you, alone. Was "secrecy" your intention? We will never know, for example, whether you ever aborted a pregnancy, loved two men at the same time, nor the nature of your dreams. Who can say when you cried, or what provoked your tears? Was your saddness related to loneliness, frustration, or depression?

I do know that they alienated you from the professional community in which you should certainly have played a more central role. I speak of your training in anthropology. Anthropology, I am sure was not ready to recognize you, a Black woman, or even your work, in its emerging canon. The more I have sought to understand you, your work, and motives, the more strongly compelled I am to search for clues to unanswered questions. But a tension exists within me—an ambivalence, it is this: What, I ask, ought to be the boundaries of inquiry? What are your rights to privacy? What of intruders, such as I must be? There is no name for this reluctance that I feel.

In the pattern of your life I see the maze of intricacies protected. I know that every life has its mysteries and secrets; photographs betray the existence of yours. There is so wide a variation in your appearance in public photographs. Each one is so unlike the others—it is almost as though each is the likeness of a different woman. A sad one. A happy one. One who appears forlorn. The tone of your skin changes, the contour of your face and body weight also vary widely. I am sure that the considerable and constant economic instability of your adult life influenced the whole of your existence. How could it be otherwise? But the "many faces of Zora" are strikingly different. I wonder whether you were a woman who wore many masks? The physically different photographed "selves" suggest an array of armours that you held up to the world. It is as though you sometimes forced yourself to smile when you felt no smile inside. Did you ponder whether you would survive out there in the world—in the wilderness—a Black woman, an unconventional Black woman? Did praise and criticism sometimes taste like the same fruit?

When all seemed futile, I know that you asked yourself whether it was all worth the sacrifice, carrying the weight of a heavy heart. Should I go forward or retreat into marriage, and "security?" Remember those photographs of yourself, turn them over in your mind, and you will recall that you appeared quite differently within short spans of time. There is the one photo that shows you wearing a wide-brimmed hat and slacks, your right foot rests on the running board of a car. Sassy! In another you pose by a fountain, hat in hand, wearing a rather pensive look—a faint smile tries to warm your face. In still another, you appear in the foreground of a scenario which includes a country house. In this one you flash a purely infectious, full-toothed smile, your head tilted slightly backward. Confident. One of those good days? A day when you tried to figure out why things went so badly yesterday, and are going so well today. The dress you will probably remember: a squared neckline, a cascade of ruffles down both sides of the bodice, all the way to the waist. The fabric is a circular print pattern. You are clutching a small handbag and wearing a sun hat. This is my favorite photograph, and obviously the favorite of many others, because it is now an available commercial postcard. The smile you wear captures all of the rays of the sun! The provocative caption under the picture reads: "She once claimed she was arrested for crossing against a red light, but escaped punishment by exclaiming that 'I had seen white folks pass on green (and) therefore assumed the red light was for me'."

*Nyazema: Where is the woman
in the moon at sunset?*

Rubbing a Paragraph with a Soft Cloth

My friend, so much is bound up in the thread of memory, real events, dreams, and myths. They . . . are not always distinguishable. Those pictures of her that you talk about; the same woman who changes every day, yet remains the same. Sometimes she looked at herself in a mirror, or at a picture, and wondered why she felt one way and *appeared* another. If you look at life as a series of hills and valleys that we must all negotiate, each in our own way, you know the truth is that you can never be sure whether you are climbing up or sliding down. Your mind may play tricks on you, and you think that down is up, and up is down. But at times that may be all you have to sustain you—that is, not knowing. Sounds strange, she knows. Our experiences, although they appear in chronological order, day after day, are not really flowing in a straight line. They are neither vertical nor horizontal, but follow the unique pattern of *one's* own hoops and life dramas. Circles within circles, some overlapping once, twice or maybe over again, and again. Complicated. All quite complicated. How might we even attempt to analyze our existence, this "upness," and "downness?" She believes that life is an uneven terrain. All the same, there is something quite natural, maybe even right, about the flow of it. Her life, your life. We never know exactly when or where the circles, loops, and dramas will intersect, obscure one another, then pale far into the distance. Another set of stars emerges and becomes the center of things. This seems to be the way it all happens. The valleys are hills, the hills, valleys.

Surely the most outstanding, the keenest recollections of one's past are those laced with the strongest emotion—great happiness, anger, love, passion, and pain. Psychic pain is what she means. Not the pain one feels in response to being struck, physically, but the pain that throbs deep down in the core of your being. A response to emotional and spiritual devastation. She wanted to tell you about her responses to a certain circumstance. Similar to Pheoby's growth experience in *Their Eyes*, our reflection could engender growth for someone, no one, or many. When it is over, we will know better how to view the sum and substance of her life. Probing this way sometimes brought pain to her heart. Not

the circles, alone, so much as our responses to them string together the totality of our lives. Vigilant introspection, and personal will compress a woman into the "self" she, ultimately, becomes. Her true self; her "woman self." There is absolutely nothing
static about a woman's life, except in tragic instances. The long
and short of it is that we are all embodiments of experiences and
beliefs that all too often have been rather indelibly imprinted
upon us. If we are fortunate, there is sufficient elasticity, and
pliability in our psyches to allow for the ruptures, shifts, and personal calamities, the constant encounters with the world of experience. If we hold on to ourselves too rigidly, or fail to flow
with the rhythm and poetry of life, and are unable to change in
the ways that our experiences dictate, the outcome is stultifica-
tion. What is important in all of this is the core of our being—who
we are inside. The center of ourselves is the point from which we
move and flex, learn and teach, find ourselves, lose ourselves,
and find ourselves again. We grow, or have the potential to do
so, bound up in experiences of growth and change.

Eatonville was Zora's center of gravity, her place in the universe; her formative, communal experience, and spiritual home.
The relationship that she had with her mother was the pivotal
one, and it oriented her like a compass to her life's path. It would
be difficult to overemphasize the importance of a nurturing community, a home, or sense of it, such as they shared in Eatonville.
She was initiated into the human family in that community and,
naturally, compared other ways of seeing the world to her
Eatonville home. Her space, a tiny dot on the globe. Her cere-
bral location, at any time, whether in South Carolina, Haiti, Jamaica, Honduras, or even taking a 1500-mile trip on her houseboat, all of the way from Florida to New York, her center was
always Eatonville. She was centered and grounded in a particular
cultural space. That early sense of personal worth derived from
home buoyed her, and "backed" her even in the community that
was Harlem—often a site of exploitative Whites and sometimes
male-focused "New Negroes." This was certainly true prior to
the incident that shook her world. Until then, it seems she had
always found the resilience and spiritual toughness to take on
the challenges that she confronted, and wrestle them, at least to
a draw. Even with the demands, humiliation, and frequent discomfort that were coexistent with her reliance on White patron-

age, she mustered the energy and courage to work. And working was the best of all possible worlds. The part of her life that she loved most. Yes, she loved herself most when she engaged in effective writing. She frequently worked in spite of physical illness and pain. Downplaying her illnesses was also a survival strategy, for she never wanted to suggest that she might be unable to work if projects were available. It was not so much a matter of trying to sustain an image of invincibility, but was more the actual need to work as often as possible. Surely, she was driven by an internal urge to write. They were organic—she and writing. They were one. Writing was the single love that she never deeply doubted: When she was not writing or working on a creative project, such as a play, or collecting tales for publication, she was grossly and insufferably miserable. Her work was her life. One unbroken line.

Whether or not she worked was the greatest barometer for determining her mood and general outlook on life. The commitment to write . . . was like a pact between her "body," and her shadow. This was a synergystic relationship that kept her relatively free from her deepest fear. That fear was a fear of personal dependence. Yet, when faced with the hard decision whether to choose love and intimacy or risk and writing, writing was, for her, the indefatigable winner. Perhaps this was an obsession related to identity, and a sense of self-worth, this piecing together of words on paper. The consummate griot? Perhaps. She avoided dependence on others who, after all, might fail or desert her. Perhaps, she simply could not trust. Simply . . . could not.

Earlier, we touched, briefly, on the political climate in America during the era of the so-called "New Negro." But there is more. When the Stock Market crashed in 1929, she was approaching her stride as a writer, readying herself for the novel because she had not yet written that challenging, sustained, peopled, narrative. She had, however, enjoyed some literary success early in the 1920s—having had published more than fifteen short stories. Additionally, she had traveled South on a couple of folklore collecting trips, and there were a few plays to her credit. In 1927 she married for the first time. This relationship did little good either for her husband, Herbert Sheen, or for Zora. The marriage was brief, lasting less than a year. Again, her love for writing had more than small influence on their lives together. Frankly, she found living the life of a *married woman* difficult. She needed physical and psychological space to engage her craft. She traveled widely in connection with her research interests and immersed herself in writing. Marriage was a big risk from the beginning. Although they had known one another a long time, more than five years, courting and living "married" they learned are quite disparate circumstances. Marriage requires different skills, and, for her, new accommodations.

They met in college, at Howard, fell in love, and continued seeing each other for a number of years. So far, so good. But the social expectations that determined, then, the nature of "marriage" impinged greatly on their ability to develop a harmonious and lasting relationship. Harmony was especially challenging to sustain because she was so often on the move researching and writing. The fact of the matter is, though, that she never wished to stay very long in anyone place, apparently, not a fact that they considered, or even felt important, as they contemplated marriage. The South and Eatonville in particular, was home, her only legitimate "community." She worked while in the North and did not really "live." By necessity, she made Harlem a quasi-home base, particularly because publishers and the Black literary coterie were situated there. Seeing the right people, having them see her in the right social settings, counted. And there were incalculable numbers of parties. Some were fun. Of course, patrons always dragged their prized Black writers off to showcase at these events when they were held downtown. For Black writers, it was New York or obscurity! Zora had to be there, at least much of the time.

Were there early doubts about the marriage? Yes. The doubts were there, hauntingly there. Despite all of this, she felt uncertain about her decision to end it. And, to complicate matters, she was irresistibly seduced by a warm climate. That seduction is now very clear to her. A warm space was always the climate of choice for work. Stories were sometimes formed—took shape in a cold climate, but their execution, their coming into the world as words on paper, required sunshine, lots of sunshine, birds flying overhead, and flowers. She never fully realized how deeply she had internalized *Mama's* dictum to "jump at the sun." The sun's energy was reviving and increased her capacity to imagine, to dream, to vivify those dreams, and make them live. She found cold weather unbearable. It was not simply an issue of temperature, but the inhabitants of cold climates seemed to have temperaments that often matched the weather. They appeared unable to thaw sufficiently to warm up to their own species. She believed, personally, that cold weather had an accumulated ill effect on the collective psyche of Black people.

Marriage . . . she can't get away from thoughts about marriage. The marriage, her first, failed on several counts. Her commitment to the marriage conflicted with her commitment to a literary career. But this was only one difficulty, a single aspect of the problem. Further, the only role he was prepared to assume was the one that named him "head of household." For her, this was a real problem. Subtly, but constantly complicating this tension was her determination to make a go of writing. She had ideas, and she wanted to preserve the culture of her youth and a particular way of living in the world. Writing is a powerful consumer of one's psychic and emotional energy. There was very little either she or he could say that would alter their situation. Nor was it possible to freely and clearly explain why she found writing essential to her existence. There was more than a little mystery there. These were difficult thoughts to convey. But because she was compelled to write, their conflict prevailed and was irreconcilable, yet virtually, nameless. Fortunately, they were not enemies at the end. They accepted the inevitable and embraced two incongruent views of life and love. They loved one another, but she also loved her work. Unfortunately, in many human situations there seem not to be the appropriately descriptive words available, those words that accurately express our thoughts and emotional dispositions. We become prisoners of our thoughts and are muted because language fails us, and we cannot convey our feelings.

Here is another way of looking at it . . . marriage. There she was in 1927, a Black woman, fledgling writer, caught between what was then thought to be two worlds. The general social expectation was that she would give up her career, just when it was really taking off. Traditional views held that she should, upon marriage, settle down, become a housewife, and, possibly, a mother. And, of course, this same expectation seemed to have been her husband's view of the marital contract. Few precedents allowed for any real emphasis on or consideration of a wife's career. Such a duality was thought to be something of a joke. The *correct* 'wife's' career was in the home. Though unwritten, this view was prevalent and powerful. You wonder why she failed to think of these things before marriage, rather than after? Of course, when two people love one another they believe that their bond is unique, the only *real* one that ever existed. They believe that their love will conquer all obstacles.

To Zora, it seemed that only a limited range of human emotion is articulable through the use of English, particularly, standard vocabulary. Therefore, the more creative forms of expression—art, literature, music, and vernacular speech, the language of the "folk"—are essential to our sense of humanness, to our ability to communicate. This is especially true of art and music, because they telescope into another realm of the human sphere and "send messages" for us to others where the spoken word fails. For her, that was the beauty of folk language. It allowed space for instant improvisation and use of a "word" never before spoken, one that provided a clear picture of the past and clarified the present. If she had had the artistic talent, she believes that she might have painted a mural on an apartment wall in Harlem to communicate messages that her words could not. Attempts to explain, to write her thoughts always seemed anecdotal. Add to this our personal and cultural unwillingness to accept the experiences of others as legitimate and filled with as much meaning as our own. Eatonville, for example, was her formative community experience. Others' notions of community, she thought, were somewhat foreign, if not inferior. She was very slow to understand and accept the lifestyles Black people lived in the North—they appeared to be sterile.

Although she lived in New York and participated in the life of the Black literary community, the level of those writers' cultural consciousness varied widely among them. There was an elite cadre and a more "common" one. W. E. B. Dubois's sensibility was the most sweeping in that he was clearly an intellectual giant and a race man who possessed a puissant artistic sensibility. Consequently, he garnered the respect of both "artist" and "intellectual" just as he was, both. For most others the separation of the artistic and the intellectual appeared more difficult. They all felt a heightened race consciousness because of DuBois's political work, not to mention the realm of personal experience. Racial antagonism against Blacks was frequent and severe. In excess of twenty race riots occurred in the early 1920s in the North. Riots were frequent in the North and Blacks were victims of lynchings in the South. Although Black writers were not an "organic" community—they held a range of beliefs about the intrinsic meaning of literature and politics separately and together, but most recognized DuBois's genius.

As for the general Black literary group in Harlem, they were all struggling with similar realities. These realities were daily sustenance and the challenge to identify publishers and audiences for their work. White patrons were key in creating publication opportunities and making essential introductions. It was not only important to have a stipend so that one might live, but there were other issues. What purpose would be served if a writer's work never reached publication? As Black writers, most struggled on at least two major fronts—one internal and related to a Black aesthetics—the other external and specifically linked to the issue of survival. And survival was clearly related to the publication of the work that they produced.

Zora was in a personal quandry, for even though she associated with most writers living in Harlem, she never experienced the kind of bonding that seemed rather commonplace between some male writers. But there was another indication of the way that values and outloook came into play at that time and not necessarily in her favor. Because she was present and obviously insisted on taking writing seriously, she found a certain level of acceptance in the Harlem writers' community and shared meaningful moments with some who were considered quite successful and some who only aspired to success. But because of profound but quiescent gender issues and a scarcity of women in the circle, she experienced little, if any, female bonding—the all important woman-to-woman friendship.

The literary community frequently viewed her with suspicion and, sometimes, amazement. She was thoroughly convinced that what was referred to as her pugnaciousness and audacity was more a reaction of shock at witnessing a woman move into an almost exclusively male domain. Their shock was not simply that she was daring enough to vigorously pursue a writing career, but that she had, pridefully, transferred her "southern" worldview and behavior from Eatonville to Harlem. She told jokes, publicly, presented rural, Black folk culture with appreciation, and extolled the beauty of authentic "Negro Spirituals." Considering the times and women's place in society, her "presence" would certainly be perceived, by many, as audacious. Perhaps it was so.

Black writers of the 1920s lived in a very unsettling era. Reconsider the fullness of the tensions that beleaguered their social world. They knew well that while Western Europe, generally, and America, particularly, suffered an economic depression in the early 1930s, these writers were more focused on establishing a literary ethos and body of literature, quite removed from prevailing national interests. The miracle was that many volumes of literature, archives of photography, paintings, and music emerged from that time that was so difficult in many ways. Nonetheless, they were determined to write prose and poetry, paint, and preserve on celluloid the social and cultural milieu that might engender respect for themselves and their race. They were willing to pay the price for such success as their projects might enjoy. While the other America experienced economic pessimism, the result of the Depression—that is, sullying of an idea about America's strength and economic viability, they were committed to the birth of a new aesthetic, a new way of representing Black life. Yes, they were caught up in their own social movement. It was the evolution of a new vision for recording the Black experience in America for generations to come.

Certainly the financial crisis finally caught up with them, in the sense that their work began to collect dust on their shelves. Philanthropy slowed to a halt, and very few former patrons were inclined to indulge in the luxury of sustaining art. For most Blacks, even food was in short supply. Jobs were even more scarce than was standard, and, eventually, the time in which this Black, avant-garde culture within a culture lived, caught them up in its web. The point, however ironic, is that as America fell deeper into financial trouble, Zora's dream of becoming an effective writer grew more vivid. She went on working with fervor, even after the Depression took hold. The national economic problem had reached Black folks uptown, and they were hit hard by it, but for many there was no place to fall. Many of old wealth, and some among the nouveau riche threw themselves from the windows of tall buildings, a result of the investment losses they had sustained. This reality affected the Black literary community in the form of patrons' skiddishness and their obvious frustration with the country's financial picture. The tempo remained upbeat in the artistic community of Harlem until around 1930.

Even more important, from the vantage point of mainstream public interest, reading Black literature was not a priority. Apart from the fact that money was scarce, a major problem for these writers and artists was the ultimate impact of the Depression on their creative edge and sensibility. While the White world struggled to right itself on its financial moorings, in the world of Black literature they tried to make their lives work against the grain of existing national crisis. Inspite of all of this Zora wrote at peak capacity between the years 1934 and 1939. She wrote well and often. There were always ideas either in her mind or on paper—oftentimes in both places. In between novels there were stories and projects and there was travel. In 1939, she married a second time.

In a sense, one might say that marriage is always one of life's main events. Yet viewing it as the major event has the potential to be misleading. Zora married Albert Price, III, in 1939, a man much younger than she. Age difference was not, however, the fundamental challenge in this relationship. She rather enjoyed marriage to a younger man. What happened? One might say that history repeated itself in the sense that her work, again, became the point of impasse. Their conflict centered around the quickly evolving expectation, on his part, that she would maintain a household and invest less energy in writing. In other words, she would write less. Again, it seemed that the arrangement ran in perfect opposition to the dominant side of her personality. She was a restless and adventursome woman. This combination of characteristics and an unyielding male perspective on marriage with regard to her writing presented them with problems familiar to her.

After all, following her mother's death, Zora became responsible for herself at an early age. Drawing together such early independence, her penchant for travel and adventure, and an abiding passion for writing, it becomes clear that there was very scant space for a "traditional" marriage. Being a woman who often needed a change of environment, likewise, she enjoyed new challenges and new scenery. Most importantly, she required a warm climate when writing. Let us face facts, Zora also bored easily.

She knows that the lens of time changes one's perspective, yet sifting through these memories, to her it seems apparent that neither marriage could ever have succeeded, if for no reason other than her persistent attitude toward writing. Her relative independence came at an early age, and she began moving around before her tenth birthday.

Also, her training in anthropology, both formal and informal, added another dimension to an essential curiosity and a zest for investigating the beliefs, values, and varied lives of others. She was aware that collecting folklore could take her to the far reaches of the globe. If the opportunity arose, the mood struck, and she could raise the money for travel, she valued the freedom to seize opportunity. These things she knew. Separation from Albert was not quite as distressing, nor as painful as the first time. She became a free woman once again and moved around as her work, mood, or circumstances permitted. Her freedom, she was learning, was as vital a part of her identity and sense of well-being as writing.

You might wonder what were the trade-offs? Aloneness and a certain vulnerability, largely related to health concerns. The obvious, one might say. Early bouts with illness were not so much frightening as they made her realize how alone she was. That realization was sometimes very disturbing, even frightening. This was especially true after the early 1940s. Although she was alone much of the time during the 1930s, she did not experience life as "a lonely woman." She had a strong inner core that gave her a sense of security—the security of the type many women seek and often find in marriage and the company of others. In one sense, she was fortunate not to have developed a dependence on others to move her through adverse situations, but instead had learned to rely on her ingenuity, intellectual resources, and internal strength. Those lessons came hard and heavy, like sheets of rain in a tropical storm after her mother's death. She lived first in one place, and then in another. Nevertheless, those hard times toughened Zora for what was to come later.

Most of the relationships that she formed in New York were directly linked to writing—they were professional, or related, in some way or another, to writing. And, yes, there were other associates outside of the literary circle. But her strongest affiliations, oddly enough, were with Black male writers. Who was tempting fate? Unfortunately, these relationships, lasted no longer than their lives were set on a common path, or a collaborative project of one kind or another.

The question she had to answer is the same many women must ask themselves: whether to seek the tenuous psychological security of home and hearth or to dive into the vast abyss of virtual independence. But she says that for her there were no deep long-lasting friendships to savor, either with women or men much of the time. The absence of connections of this nature were most painfully missed when her health seriously failed. But she had made certain choices about her life and understood their consequences. Friendship requires an investment of time, energy, give and take, and the will to succeed. In this way, friendship is like marriage. Yet, these are the identical prerequisites to productive writing. Furthermore, one must desire long-term relationships, a lesson that she missed, not so much by choice, but because of the unsettled, and unsettling pattern of her early life.

There was little security in Zora's life from the age of nine through her early twenties. Yes, she was on her own during those crucial growth years, those years when young girls learn what it means to develop friendships and to understand the value of female friendship. Those associations usually begin around the same age that she was essentially orphaned and her ability to develop friendships would never fully develop. In this situation there were both advantages and disadvantages. Intellectually and even emotionally she understood the need for, and the nature of friendship between women. She observed them among the women in Eatonville and expressed a profound knowledge of the role that such relationships might play in women's lives as evidenced in *Their Eyes*. Janie's influence on Pheoby's growth is nothing less than phenomenally powerful.

Because she chose a male-dominated profession, the few women who might have otherwise been good friends were competitors for the same grants, awards, and philanthropic handouts that she sought. There, little space was available to men or women, and certainly there would never be very many women that males would allow, then, to compete at their level.

When a woman decides to live her life without a male at its center and complicates the matter by choosing as her life's work a profession in which ill winds often blow, she will face retribution for her transgression—for going against social expectations of "good" female behavior. In this choice making, a major sacrifice she had to consider was the supreme possibility of the loss of enduring relationships with women. For Zora the matter was made more complex by others' constant focus on her *behavior* rather than on her work. Social isolation from her own kind was an outcome of that critique. If a woman is without deep relationships and close friends, who might be aware if she was harmed or incapacitated in some way? This was a problem that she faced.

In the view of most she was on the periphery of the Black literary world, living in a state of perpetual marginality. This means that her every infraction of "right behavior" was sufficient to cause the critical establishment to isolate her or threaten to banish her from that community. Critiques such as this were usually the result of an opinion about either her actual or literary voice. And only after she had served her time in isolation—missing parties and other gatherings—was she allowed to rejoin the literary community. It was her opinion that few vocal and productive women escape extreme scrutiny of their personal lives and the vicissitudes of public opinion.

The problem is related to the world of larger social issues. It's the old bear trap. Certain social expectations for men, others for women. In America, for example, there can be only one "official" head of household—the Census Bureau supports that notion in the way that questions are framed to arrive at national population statistics. On the data collection form there is a category: "Head of Household," and, "Single, Head of Household," or something like that. The point, though, is that only when there is an adult female living without a man in the house, might she be considered "responsible" or "head." No consideration is given to the notion of shared adult authority. There must be a "leader." The thinking here and the language that is its result are problematic. When two adults live together, why must one be designated as "head?" What is corrupt about the designation, "Co-heads of Household?" In any case, this type of social role designation creates injustices for both women and men.

First of all, the designation "head" is based primarily on an income index and a political position. It is supposed to be a determinant of which of the two adults has the largest income. One result of the existing structure is that the social system provides larger remuneration for working males than for working females in comparable situations. This arrangement supports the relegation of women to subservient positions in workplaces. The "political power" established in the social world is most often lived out in the home. The problem, though, is that while they are discouraging working and non-working women, both by direction and indirection, they also devalue the critical role she plays in the home, which is then played out within society.

Zora would agree with those who believe that child rearing, and taking care of the sick and aged, are among the few profoundly humanizing and character-building experiences left in the world. The overwhelming number of people who perform these tasks are women. But there is no reason that these humanizing opportunities should be envisioned, solely, as the province of women. After all, women have only *learned* the role of care giver.

With this notion of "Head of Household" in mind, where do you place the man who, for legitimate reasons, cannot locate employment but shares the household with a working woman and perhaps provides primary care for his children. Such a man, and the familial constellation to which he belongs will suffer social stigma that is directly related to the implications of the category "Head of Household." He is unable to fit into the box or wear the label. And, of course, when one looks at the Black community, in every part of America, and around the world, forces external to the community have sketched the blueprint for what are appropriate social arrangements. These guidelines may or may not accurately depict the realities of many non-majority, immigrant people in America.

Had Zora's desire to pursue writing been deemed "appropriate" then perhaps—just perhaps—one of her intimate relationships might have at least begun with a different premise, a different set of parameters and possibilities. In fact, she did talk about the way that her work became a bone of contention in relationships with the men she married. The very notion of her professional life was unacceptable, and their mindset on this issue was rooted in values established by the mainstream, even though they belonged to a historicially marginalized community. Her outspokenness was exacerbated not only by gender, but also by her status as an unmarried woman, or a woman who was married for only brief periods. And this reality, again, had its natural extension in the world of logic. Unmarried, she was quite limited in the number of women of similar circumstances and interests with whom she could identify. More than being unmarried, her attitude towards the institution seemed threatening. Had there been more women writing, she would have had a wider range of dispositions and perspectives from which to extend and receive friendship—some of which may have corresponded with hers. It is possible that she would have shared the status of her health with friends and perhaps received encouragement and advice.

For a time she confided in Carl Van Vechten but later saw the precarious nature of that relationship and the role that he played—stoking the fire—in her disagreement with Langston Hughes. But choices were few. Among Black men who, like Zora, struggled to survive in the tenuous world of the "literati," certainly few felt secure enough to support and encourage her sometimes wilted spirit. And, she questioned whether or not she was sufficiently open and trusting. Yet, somehow the men managed to include male bonding in the scope of their experiences, she concluded, to a definite advantage. Arna Bontemps's and Langston Hughes's friendship is a perfect example of long-term male bonding. Theirs, it seems, was a lasting, reciprocal relationship, while her connection with Hughes, although once close, ended abruptly and with bitterness.

Friends are helpful in so many ways—good to have. For one thing, they monitor one another's behavior, in both the public and private spheres. As mentioned before, she often appeared quite differently in photographs in that the manner of her dress and countenance varied widely. Certainly, comparing photographs over time, growing older meant increasing weight control problems that might cause a notable difference. The fluctuation in her body weight had a negative effect on her health, resulting eventually in serious health problems. Towards the end of the 1930s she was given to turns of over-eating followed by a normal appetite. The problem was related to stomach pain and distress. Whenever the stomach problem became active, she could hardly imagine ever again over-eating. So her facial expression was affected by internal conditions and external realities, such as the absence of financial means. If things were reasonably tranquil inside—meaning that there was an absence of stomach pain, and she was making her way, financially, she usually appeared just as she felt—cheerful and outgoing. On the other hand, if life appeared bleak, and she lacked the resources to meet financial obligations—pay bills, purchase food and clothing—her facial expression betrayed these controlling factors. The world was put on notice that Zora had fallen on hard times. For Black writers, then, there was no means to settling matters such as this for all time. Sometimes she was on top of her affairs, at others she was uncertain whether she would make it to the next oasis in a vast desert. This was the contour of existence, then, for most Black writers. The literary world appeared to be a lush tropical forest that magnetized her. She was thirsty for all of its nectar. Occasionally, even when her health and financial outlook were grim, she mustered a large, toothy grin. Those were the smiles of an imposter. Sheer pretense.

The most dependable measure of Zora's state of mind was the ease or difficulty she felt while writing. When all was well, and her spirit high, she often imagined that she could complete a book in a single sitting. Words presented themselves, adeptly, out of her reservoir of images. Chaste memories, some delicious, others bitter. There was little need to dredge. Language, scenes, and characters sometimes appeared unceremoniously, at other times with great color and fanfare. Themes and countless variations rushed through her mind—endless, endless rivers of crystal clear thought. When she was ill or distressed, writing a few acceptable pages felt like an eternity. Her last known effort, which she began in 1953, *Herod the Great,* and with which she wrestled, yet never completed, is the ultimate example of strife in her literary life. The work was simply too difficult. . . . She wrote in very poor health, in a state of physical and psychic pain without a promise of publication. She wrote over a period of years, and yet she could not complete the work in a manner acceptable to her publisher. How might things have gone had she not suffered both physical and spiritual crises? She is unsure, not certain, and cannot say. At that time—during those years—the 1950s, she felt diminished. She attempts to say that most of the words that she put on paper seemed hollow and lifeless. The failure of the *Herod* work did not diminish her. It was the fault of those whose agenda it was to bring her down. Desperation. She had begun feeling a sense of desperation. She was swimming, yet sensed that the water was too deep.

Rebounding in her life—how many times? Zora was well trained to stay afloat in a rough sea. There had been times during her youth after her mother's death when she wandered around and worked for Whites in kitchens. She prevailed and existed by sheer wit and will. The most frightening test of her will to survive had come early. Yes, it was her mother's death that put her survival dexterity in motion. In real terms, she was very much a child then.

There was yet another test of her will in the academic world: Morgan Academy, in Maryland, Howard University, in Washington, D.C., and Barnard in New York. Ultimately, before her lay the challenge of survival in the literary world, the world of "New Negro" consciousness. She came through all of these challenges, and she endured until tragedy struck her spirit at unfathomable depth. The world deepened in darkness and perceptiveness, and sensibility blunted. This darkness and despair that she lived was strangling and could only disrupt her work. This reality was to soon become obvious to others.

In a way she was more advantaged than some because they identified with and drew their creative energy, sustenance, and inspiration from contemporary urban Black life—specifically, from Harlem. By that she means that few of her contemporaries relied consistently, and to the same extent as she, on southern folk tradition for their material. And, certainly there were those who questioned the appropriateness of placing southern Black traditional culture at the center of a new literary consciousness that became a social movement with international reach. Indeed, the literature and implicit politics of that period in Harlem inspired similar forms of expression in the Caribbean and in Europe. Some might have argued that others used southern Black culture and tradition in their work more effectively than she.

The study of social science acquainted Zora with the high value placed on "objectivity," and the alleged dangers inherent in the researcher coming too close to the subject. The implication here is not that others' work was dispassionate or estranged from the realities of Black life. She merely suggests that this "objectivity" is difficult to achieve, no matter how close one is to, or distant from, the subject. We carry troublesome biases, even in science. There might be some benefit to admitting their presence. Collecting "folktales," as her *Mules and Men* suggests, was akin to replaying scenes from her youth. Yet, in some instances collecting was filled with profoundly new experiences, as is obvious in *Tell My Horse*. It was her belief that the people from whom stories were collected enjoyed "performing," as much as she did hearing and recording them. Once the group began talking, the "lies" fell smoothly from their tongues, and they fought for a chance to speak, to influence a "group project."

Nevertheless, by the time her *Moses* book was published in 1939, Zora had written diligently for nearly twenty years and was quite as poor then as when she started. She believed this to be the consequence of double jeopardy: being a Black woman with an opinionated voice. Poverty and illness set the stage for despair and for the darkness and the spiritual dissonance. She was more than mildly disillusioned by all of this. The ultimate realization that she would never earn a decent living gained momentum as her grimmest reality. Would she ever enjoy full membership in her professional community? Rather, it seemed that she would always be subject to unfavorable critiques. Their criticism was not so much focused on her work but on interpretations of her personal life. The malevolence was related to her expectation that she move through the world with the ease of men—obviously, misalignment of social expectations. The political views that she expressed were, generally, attacked. Contending with social pique, chronic illness, and debilitation in her middle years became an awesome burden. There is uncertainty whether she was either willing or able to accept the reality of aging and physical degeneration. Zora did not take the best care of herself. She enjoyed highly seasoned food and never really felt inclined to worry about nutrition. This lack of attention figured prominently in the additional pounds that she took on at middle age.

Around the mid-1940s she noticed that her energy level was falling considerably below normal—not what it was before, for as long as she could remember. The same amount of energy expended to write no longer yielded the same results. Noting the slowdown in her productivity, others wondered whether she would continue a creative life. She was encouraged by her publisher, for a long time, to write an autobiography but had resisted. Bearing her soul was not something that she looked forward to or even desired doing. But by 1941 she decided to write the autobiography, in part, because times were so tough. Certainly, she omitted certain events in her life and shrouded others. There was considerable rewriting of sections. Some of this rewriting was due to pressures from her publisher and from her patron.

She was also unsure of the impact of the political climate on readers' interpretation of her life writing. Therefore, she believed her best interest would be served if the book was both open *and* closed. But *Dust Tracks* contains many truths that may only be perceived by the deeply insightful reader. In the final analysis she would agree that certain aspects of the book *appear* rather prosaic, but the reader should not ignore those truths that are revealed. Her personal problem with the general way the book was received has to do with her thought about what she saw as the general population's desire to know the entire and absolute details of the private lives of public personalities. Quite candidly, she favored a modicum of privacy for all. Nevertheless, *Dust Tracks*, was her most acclaimed work. The early 1940s were tough—no money, unproductive. She felt compelled, by circumstances, to write what she believed might move her towards security—a means to sustain life. *Dust Tracks*, although thought to be convoluted to some and empty to others, was laced with essential honesty, particularly, the portion concerning her youth. She felt it important and beneficial to write about her early life, and to do so outside the framework of fiction. Certain other aspects of her life she sometimes treated in the framework of the latter. About *Dust Tracks*, she earnestly believed that those who might read the book would do so without particular commentary, due to the way the work is written—rather, simplistically, at the surface . . . on the face of it. She quite carefully set up the book's outline, the frame for the book. By doing so, she could better control the flow of information, guarding against the tendency to write emotionally. *Dust Tracks* is not that type of revelation. That is, the book is not a "lay open your soul" autobiography. Further, it seemed then that she ought not to offend those who might purchase the book. So, indeed, she removed sections that were overtly political—especially her thoughts about U.S. imperialism towards the Japanese.

In fact, from the *Moses* work forward, her fiction was directed away from Black life to some degree. Prior to *Moses*, she purposely wrote directly toward Blacks, although they were not, necessarily, the audience who would comprise the greatest number of readers. Writing out of a particular Black experience, she hoped to show the richness of southern folk culture, and even preserve that culture in history. In retrospect, the impact of her work on the White world, as far as she could tell, was virtually nil.

She completed only one other novel after the autobiography—
Seraph on the Suwanee, published in 1948. *Seraph* did not, primarily, concern the Black condition. Its focus was White
southerners. Neither did the book receive high critical acclaim,
although it appealed to some. In the final analysis, then, *Seraph*
was nearly a total failure, in the critics' view. Between *Moses* and
Seraph, her life was spongy and filled with much unpleasantness.

Zora held a teaching position in Durham, South Carolina from
1940 to 1941; that was a somewhat unsuccessful encounter in
that she was at odds with the College Director because of his
general attitude toward education. At the same time, her short
marriage to Albert Prince was falling apart, for they had unsuc-
cessfully attempted reconciliation. In the view of some, the relationship left a trail of suspicion in its wake. The suspicion had to
do with a woman marrying a man much younger than herself,
together with her earlier unsuccessful relationships. Add to that
the sentiment held by her detractors that she was spent as a
writer. Therefore, Zora's problem was not so much one of creative bankruptcy, as it was the aggregated effect of her total life
picture: crumbling personal relationships, ill health, poverty, de-
spondence, and spiritual crisis. Her life was in a steady state of
decline. Remembering . . . now reflecting, she knows that her
stresses were closely interrelated to her constant confrontation
with her marginal status—her existence at the edge for so long.
Ultimately, the combination of the whole of her life, apart from
the research, fieldwork, and writing, exacted a great personal
toll. She felt then, too, a sense of failed potential as a writer, but
realized that the prospect for rising to that pinnacle was very,
very bleak.

Aging and quite poor, her health worsened with every year,
and the writing once so thoroughly enjoyed, almost to the point
of ecstasy, began to wane to less than a casual interest. The result of a national economic Depression, the slow climb uphill
towards literary recognition, combined with a lost love, weighed
ever so heavily. Perhaps it was unreasonable to assume that pleasure reading about Black life might find popularity in a time when
the salient issue, before so many, was survival. At first, she was
merely a woman alone, trying to understand what went wrong.
She would rapidly become an unhappy, sometimes angry, sick
woman, now more alone than ever.

There was so much despair and so little human caring. She was deeply perplexed by the consternation that humans exhibited toward one another. Perhaps what now appeared to be a human tendency of enmity toward one another had always been there. Had she existed, lived in the world oblivious to such a presence? New York City, Harlem, the environment where she had, at least, developed professionally, to a degree, became a breeding ground for her despondency. She decided that the best therapy for her would be Florida sunshine. She returned home, symbolically, to peace, acceptance, and security. Trips to Florida would soon become a ritual of healing, and she took as many trips South as she could muster financially. The warmth was sustaining and shrunk her innermost despair.

In 1943 she moved to Daytona Beach and bought a houseboat. Living on the water was a good way to come to terms with herself and the world. She adored the experience—life filled with sunshine and the lush greenery that it produces. Her houseboat ("Wagano") was a source of renewal, and rejuvenation for four wonderful years. She returned to New York only when business required that she do so. "Business," in the way spoken of here means attempts at earning money to make ends meet and to extend life at her water paradise.

In contrast, life on the boat contributed greatly to her happiness—more pleasing than anything she had ever dreamed possible. Living on the water, in Florida, felt so different. This was the polar opposite of her existence in New York. Such a peaceful, relaxing hiatus. Perhaps, there was more to the inner accord that she felt than was obvious. From her study of the religious practices and beliefs among Blacks in New Orleans and the Caribbean, she understood the occult beliefs attached to large bodies of water—among other meanings, they are symbolic representations of spiritual renewal and rebirth. But her euphoria and the absence of depression were also rooted in her love of the outdoors. She had, earlier, planted a flower and vegetable garden in Eau Galle. Living in this environment, she breathed clean, fresh air, fished, and travelled from harbor to harbor, and passed the time of day with others who also appreciated this slowed-down pace. Life, then, was spiritually regenerative—it was just the medicine that she had needed. The weather was warm, the sun shone daily. Uplifting! Also comforting was the proof that she could create, for herself, on her own, a sense of well-being. There was genuine self-initiated contentment within her reach. She recalls that in 1943, an executive of the NAACP charged her with a lack of integrity in an article that appeared in the *Amsterdam News*. He suggested that Zora would do anything to sell books. The not so hidden message was that Zora Neale Hurston was a big sell-out—that she used Blacks. She was deeply wounded by the charge, particularly considering the source. The NAACP executive's anger, and negative critique was fueled by an earlier comment that she made and that was published in the February 1 edition of the *New York World Telegram*. In the statement, Zora said that Blacks were better off in the South than they were in the North.

Many of her colleagues and others in the North pointed the finger at the South as the only part of the country where Blacks were racially oppresssed. Life in the North assured her that the oppression of Blacks was not a regional issue but a national one. As she grew to a clear understanding of the intractable nature of race-based oppression in America, North and South she was no longer perplexed by the failure of "democracy." In her 1945 essay, "Crazy for this Democracy," she satirizes the race problem. Her essay was poorly received by Whites and met the resentment of several Blacks in the critical community. There was a growing awareness, on her part, about why Blacks often attack one another. She considered that Blacks empower the negative images that others paint of us, and then internalize them, and strike out at mirror images of ourselves. Bemoaning this sad circumstance, she regretted it all, for life is so much larger than "race," far more than color.

In fact, her personality was the major critical focus among many of the "New Negroes" in Harlem suggested as the reason she was less successful than she might otherwise have been were she disposed to managing herself "appropriately." Blacks in America, generally though, are recipients of a similar brand of criticism. As a group, they are challenged to disprove charges of laziness, dishonesty, and violence. These labels are attached to the entire race. The challenge that she faced among her Black critics, was to prove them wrong—an impossible fete to achieve. For what she perceived to be their faulty judgment, would have only been translated into more lampooning. The entrapment here, as in the case with race, is that "it's your own fault that you can't make the grade." In Zora's situation, the suggestion was that had she just not been such an "aggressive," and "mouthy" woman—settled down with one of those men who breathed heavily in her ear, her misfortune would have been avoided. The suggestion is, obviously, that "good" girls avoid "bad" outcomes. Continuing that line of thought, one could surmise that she would have been "protected."

She pondered and thought of the women that she knew who displayed "good behavior," and could recall few who were cared for in old age by men. But that was the story that she simply had ruined her own chance for real happiness—divorcing husbands and not knowing what was best for herself. There was something grossly awry with that scenario, and it stuck in her gut. Her hunch was later borne out when in 1959 she was forced by poverty and destitution to move into a welfare settlement in Ft. Pierce, Florida. Welfare. Yes, her life would come to that. Zora received public welfare and was forced to move in with other aged, ill, and poor Black women. Many of these women had been married for many years, and, yet, there was no one around to care for them. Unlike hers, most of those women's lives were politically "correct."

She thought once during an unusually lengthy stay in New York that doldrums were permanently with her and maybe she could never feel her "old self" again. Perhaps, the power to renew from within was lost. The other side of the story was that a burgeoning political sophistication, maturity, and her personal circumstances brought affirmation that the social condition of Blacks was deeply entrenched in American culture. In her early writing race was downplayed and culture was the central focus. Now, she realized that there was a much clearer and more profound relationship between the two. Painfully, she realized that she was only slightly better off in more economically stable times because her marginal status extended far beyond the purely economic. In fact, her incipient poverty reinforced a set of truths that had already been revealed. These were truths that she once attempted to discount.

These revelations were directly related to the long hours of work, the running around with, and cajoling patrons, acquiescing to their whims and fancies. They were, more often than not, exceedingly controlling individuals. But there she was, years later, still poor. In hindsight, the compromises were not worth the price she paid, not for a hand-to-mouth existence. At the same time she realized that patronage had afforded her the joy and contentment that only writing could provide. But now she was engaged in a protracted struggle to save herself. All that had made life worth living, although challenging was slipping from her grasp.

In her later years she was keenly aware of the central place of writing to her mental and spiritual well-being. The sacrifices made in the service of writing had to be viewed in that light. Apart from what she hoped was its intrinsic social value, writing was a critical practice in her life for the way that it opened her to self-discovery, self-reflection, and healing. Through the vehicle of her literary voice, Zora moved back and forth between worlds—the cherished past world of her youth—home, family, and community. Those thoughts seem to have brought back the life with her mother. Her literary voice was also important for its explorative power of other peoples' cultures and their different beliefs and practices. Writing, she understood, had provided the balance in her life. Beyond a doubt, it was the generative and regenerative force of her adulthood.

Zora writes succinctly in *Dust Tracks* about the place and primacy of writing: "I have come to know by experience that work is the nearest thing to happiness that I can find. No matter what else I have among the things that humans want, I go to pieces in a short while if I do not work. What all my work shall be, I don't know that either, every hour being a stranger to you until you live it. . . ."

Like a sacred form of inscription—something akin to Haitian VeVe—writing was mysteriously prescriptive in the way that a "medicinal concoction" works within the body of the sick. While immersed in the practice, she became a priestess who had the power to summon gods, goddesses, and Yoruba divine spirits (Iwa). When so empowered by writing, she could ignore everyday annoyances. Therefore, the loss of her power to summon "words" was wholly disempowering and degenerative for her.

Zora had suffered a serious gall bladder attack in 1945 and that illness caused her to wonder whether she would ever again be physically well. Had she come to the beginning of the end? Attempting to be brave, she superficially contemplated facing old "square toed" death for the first time. She regained a semblance of health over the next few years but would never again be really free from mild to severe abdominal distress. One problem was related to the fact that during most of her research travel outside the country she consumed a wide variety of food that often irritated her stomach condition. Furthermore, she later suffered pain and fever caused by an infection she contracted by drinking contaminated water in Honduras, during a trip there in 1952. Interestingly, exceptions to her typical pattern of food indulgence occurred only during periods of intense writing. At such times she was totally engaged, concentrated on the work at hand, and held few thoughts about food. So, obviously, as she worked less over longer periods, frustrated, she consumed more—the result of tension and uncertainty about the future.

By the time she began to feel quite ill, she was also just about as angry as could be because of the events that were and were not occurring in America. Simultaneously, she realized that she might just as well write and speak her mind and be done with it. Things were already bad for her and worse for most Blacks. So she did just that—spoke and wrote her conscience. She felt free when she wrote articles and essays on the way that America is governed and expounded on every subject that troubled her. Nearly everything she wrote was uncomplimentary. She was also as mad as hell that America had not allowed her the comfort of contributing what she knew about Black culture without stress and strain. And, she doubted that anyone would look back at her work in the future, and few listened when she discussed what, in her opinion, was wrong with America. Even Blacks objected to what she had to say.

Considering that, she let go of whatever was on her mind and it felt right. She talked about the North not being a haven of justice and argued that the North had never had racial justice at all. Another of her topics was relationships between individual Blacks and Whites, and her belief that many Blacks have a few "special" Whites who are, they believe, exceptions to prototypical insulting White conduct and behavior towards Blacks. In her essay on democracy she wrote that America attempts to overpower and dominate cultures that are different from her own. In "The Pet Negro System" she commented that just as Blacks have "special White friends" Whites, too, have "pet Negroes." She doubted that any of what she spoke or wrote was earth-shattering, or even news, especially among Black writers in Harlem. Indeed, she and her associates, Blacks and Whites, participated in these racial games, in one way or another. What then of improved race relations?

Zora vented by the written and the spoken word on the topic of the "racial monster." Perhaps, to the surprise of few, she was even sufficiently unladylike to sometimes name names. Some of those who were thought to be "Blackest," who talked about Whites as though they were angels were called by name, as were those who, contrarily, believed Whites to be endowed with tails and stripes. When she examined a majority of her associations, she discovered that they were rather, uniformly, unpredictable— sometime victims, others victimizers.

Retrospectively, she is clear about the fact that after the early 1940s most of her writing was, in essence, definitively polemical. She went "out on a limb," and dared to write a novel about Whites—her last published one, *Seraph.* Common opinion was that the book was little more than an attempt to prove that she was not limited to the space of retelling the lives of the "folk" in Eatonville and other rural southern communities. Maybe the criticism of her capacity to write beyond the familiar was an unconscious motivation for *Seraph.* But at the level of the conscious, she felt the need to delve into the lives of the dominant culture, to look at White relationships as one way of demystifying Whiteness.

Certainly, she may also have hoped that the new subject matter, or subject matter new to her fictional repertoire, would eliminate some of the pessimism and doubt that clouded portions of her earlier work. This, then, would be a new beginning. A rash of troubles presented themselves as she attempted to see *Seraph* published by Lippincott. One difficulty was related to her desire to travel to Honduras in search of a lost Mayan city. The one certainty was that she yearned to travel there, or elsewhere, where the weather was warm, the scenery lush, so that she might bring her writing of Seraph to an end. Zora needed to move close to nature so that she could complete this project. And, she earnestly wanted to explore the Mayan ruins. A lover of adventure, the Honduras idea seemed sensational and appealed to her for the possibility it held to unravel hundreds of years of mystery. Information she had gathered suggested that only one person ever had set eyes on the Mayan city. If she could get there, write, and research the culture, the trip would be one of tremendous importance. Not only might she have an opportunity to recast history in a new and creative motif, but it presented an extraordinary opportunity to bring together anthropological theory and practice.

She vacillated, dropped the idea, and picked it up again—applied for a Guggenheim but was rejected. In the meantime, she organized a community self-help project for Black mothers and their children in Harlem. Not long after getting the self-help program underway, her luck changed, and Scribners paid her $500 to continue work on *Seraph*. She sailed for Honduras in May 1947. Her health was not the greatest, but she felt driven and thought that the travel and adventure might be good, perhaps healing. The book was published by Scribners in October 1948.

Zora believed that her training in anthropology had beeen used effectively and creatively in view of the way that she structured the presentation of folklore, tales, and mythology recorded in *Mules and Men* and *Tell My Horse*. In other words, the formal training she received in anthropology was a useful analytical device for various aspects of her research. Whether culture is explored for its use in fiction or folklore, the most significant aspects of the subjects' lives—their worldview and their view of themselves in the world—it was all there in these works. For Zora, storytelling and myth are the substance of which novels "speak," embellished by the imagination. She perceived little significant difference, that is substantive difference, between writing ethnography and writing fiction. They might be thought of as obverse sides of the same coin. The ethnographer would likely be constrained to write herself out of the work; the novelist writes, unconstrained, from a space within her reservoir of emotion. Both are interpretive literary forms, although one is thought to be "science" and the other "art."

In many ways the corpus of the work that she produced was strongly ethnographic, whether fiction or folklore, for the fact that her work presented cultural images of Black life authenticated by both her lived experience and participant observation in various communities in the rural South. Of course some would argue that she held a built-in bias for what she believed to be the superior cultural motif of the southern way. In other words, she lacked "objectivity." But under what circumstances does one enter a new environment without cultural baggage?

What about the influence of cultural and personal change and maturation on her work? As she looked across the years predating the publication of her last novel, Zora was keenly aware of the changes that occurred in her life, in her personality, and in her view of the world. As the polemical essays she wrote in the 1940s and 1950s intone, over time she had become more the realist—one who understood the global connection among Blacks. This awareness in no way contradicted the cultural experiences that she had earlier vaunted. Parallel to that insight, there was an ongoing assessment of her life experiences as a woman, singularly, and as a participant in a literary movement that was a special moment in time. Her life as a "Black female writer" actually politicized her more definitively than she had realized until circumstances forced personal reflection. She was, of course, always aware of the racial hierarchy in America but gave little credence to the notion that the dominant culture would not change towards Blacks. Of course, her early emphasis privileged gender, not race. Likewise, her assessment of the problems Blacks had in society was grounded in what she believed to be a general lack of knowledge on the part of Whites to understand Black tradition and cultural bounteousness. She believed, further, that Blacks often related negatively to one another because of a lack of knowledge of the historical past. In other words, Blacks had come to believe the negative myths about ourselves, particularly, those that emerged out of slavery in the West.

As she came to grips with her reality, Zora no longer was to be denied her sense of the reach of "politics" into the life she lived. She had been a prolific writer despite hardships and personal distresses. These facts notwithstanding, she had never overcome life on the edge—life with the bare necessities or less. She grew angry and pained. The impact of a deeper truth, that is that Blacks seemed relegated to a mythologized past that could not be risen above by demonstrated competence, skill, or intellectual capacity raised her anger and promoted a more open and political didacticism. The aspirations and dreams that she dreamed had been short-circuited. Yes, she tasted mediocre success but never the personal triumph nor the cultural exaltation that she and other Black writers had worked hard to achieve.

As for her peers, men such as Wallace Thurman, Claude McKay, Langston Hughes, and Alain Locke, she was one of few among that coterie of Harlem writers who, while often traveling to the Caribbean, researching and writing from formerly colonized Black countries (Haiti, Jamaica, Honduras), remained unseduced by Paris and the European scene. She was aware of the impact of her peers' interactions with Martinicans and Senegalese in Paris, and their influence on emergent literary movements, such as Negritude, in these countries. The inspiration that they provided proved to be historically significant. Yet, she had no regrets about the literary and political decisions she made.

Zora was honest enough with herself to allow that she sustained an extra portion of critical judgments because of gender and suspected that the few other women who moved in a sphere, typically male, did also. But she believed that she had proved herself hardy and had produced alongside the best of men, gender notwithstanding. It seemed reasonable, too, to believe that her capacity for the craft of writing, her independence, and her desire to care for herself might be valued. In the final analysis it appears that her self-sufficiency and refusal to whimper were useless if not detrimental characteristics.

Would her peers have thought her to be an "authentic" woman had she validated the social blueprint for what a "real" woman was supposed to do and be? Does this question contradict itself? The prevailing sentiment among Zora's peers seemed to suggest that because she viewed herself to be different from the majority of women—having chosen "men's work"—she should simply have to suffer the consequences of that choice. The consequences, in this instance, mean whether or not she should be included among the legitimate Black literati. Most among them remained somewhat circumspect on this issue for the entire period of her association with these writers despite a few collaborative works. That she appeared unwilling to internalize their authority to validate either her presence or work was for them even more maddening and provocative.

The various dimensions of Zora's long-term marginal status began to congeal by the late 1950s. The sun provided temporary healing and energy, and she followed it to the extent allowed by meager financial resources. She even found writing slipping slowly from her grasp and sphere of pleasure. All appeared lost. Without her work she was certain that all was lost. How would she recapture and reinvigorate her spirit? What would it take to erase the monster living behind her eyes? The "self" that she was becoming seemed, at first, incompatible with memories of what she was once. Uncertainty crowded her and became all too familiar, all too debilitating. The irony in all of this was that she sensed a meshing of the old Zora with the new. Nonetheless, she dreaded it and fought against herself—an attempt to stave off the change and emergence of the new and unfamiliar—yet, strangely, she also welcomed its prospect.

In those days she thought often of the story of Janie Mae Crawford and revisited Janie's and Phoeby's experiences of change and transformation. She remembered thinking and writing: "Years ago, she had told her girl self to wait for her in the looking glass. It had been a long time since she had remembered. . . . She went over to the dresser and looked hard at her skin and features. The young girl was gone, but a handsome woman had taken her place." Zora's awareness turned slowly and awkwardly inward toward the great struggle that was taking place there. She could name the struggle—it was "resistance"—to change, aging, and an emergent form of enlightenment. She wondered whether this form of resistance was no more than a human characteristic. If so, what might this mean, for example, for race progress? She saw herself as a reflection of society—an abhorrent and invidious reflection. Her insight now crystallized, but with whom would she share these visions? There was no Phoeby. Waiting for a period, she recentered herself. But so much had happened that had damaged her physical and spiritual health, and much of the damage was irreversible. Zora mentally shuffled through old encounters and experiences and pondered the early years in New York. She thought about former relationships. She concluded that the most meaningful of her personal interactions, even when brief, were those in which there was space for her to simply be, to exist as herself, express her thoughts and opinions, and explore issues. The best were those that allowed her to talk about her work and others'. Perhaps because there was little that was personal at stake in most of those old relationships she had felt a genuine sense of freedom and élan. Retrospectively, she saw herself so often railing against boundaries wherever they existed in her life, under whatever guise they assumed. Certain relationships were fundamentally objectionable because of others' need to see her in the role of a "traditional" woman. They lauded her, for example, the "good cook," but cared less about the "writer" in her spirit—the writer that was her life.

As mentioned before, Zora threw parties when her financial situation allowed, not expensive parties, rather, small gatherings that, sometimes, expanded. On those occasions her associates were invited to join her for large pots of food, which she prepared with delight. Her objection to "housewifery" was not related to not knowing her way around a kitchen. But many preferred the Zora in the kitchen, or the image of a woman's place, that made them most comfortable. This was the part of her that was least threatening. A woman stirring a pot on a stove is a righteous image.

Bearing the scars of many battles she was keenly aware that they were fought against a system on two levels—race and gender. Tired, poor, and ill, she was uninspired and struggled with her writing. The stark awareness of the consequences of her race and gender was, in political terms, weighty. Though her early literary and folkloric emphasis held a strong bias in favor of culture rather than race, her personal predicament made clear the many wounds and challenges of the past. Gender was a politically potent though often silent issue for the Black critical establishment. Race was more an issue among publishers, patrons, and the reading public. Yet, in a certain way the lines were not so clearly drawn and often merged, spilling over one onto the other. Because the images that peopled her novels and short stories might have been viewed by her critics as caricatures, or little more than figments of an overdrawn imagination, it was easier to dismiss them as just so many images conjured up in the head of a "strange" Black woman. But this emergent, polemical Black woman grew in her psyche and, like Janie Mae Crawford, strained to achieve freedom and wholeness.

Unrelenting poverty notwithstanding, in her later years Zora embodied certain dimensions of reward for time that she invested in grappling with survival and personal sacrifice. No doubt, she was sustained while in the clutches of many known and unknown adversaries by remembering the early loss of her mother. These thoughts were oddly strengthening. She also understood that her own strong need for control and autonomy were related to her mother's death. In other words, she suffered an identity crisis with the loss of her mother who was her mirror. Having been ordered by her father and other adults to cover the mirror at her mother's death, against her mother's wishes and her own, Zora felt helpless. The adults' insistence upon covering the mirror also symbolically obscured Zora's self-image, which she was driven to recover. Similarly, Janie's true identity, a fit between her shattered inner self and outer reality, was the crux of her personal struggle. For Zora and for Janie, these struggles were initially disconcerting but ultimately enabling. The shape of her life and love and the adversities she overcame created a new woman in Janie. A woman who reassembled the broken pieces of herself to become whole.

Zora's mature years were, therefore, a time of intense spiritual reflection, healing, and transcendence. But there was a process and an order to her metamorphosis. She recognized the multifarious nature of her problems and the ways that race, gender, and assumed societal intransigence are generational. Generations of Black women, since slavery, have inherited a legacy of a certain type of injustice—sometimes, subtle injustice—a preinscribed place in the American system. But Zora also made the erroneous assumption that the lack of knowledge might be at the heart of these assumptions. Therefore, as truths were revealed, and Black literature would be a major reservoir of truth, attitudes would change towards the race, and Black women might be judged as individuals.

Zora's response to this emergent "self," nonetheless, produced polemical articles and critical essays on Blacks, generally, and others related to her personal experience. Poorer Black women, women who were even poorer than she, caused her outrage, as well. Realization of the connection between her consciousness and literary voice was a powerful one. The social and political ramifications attached to speaking versus denial and silençe were troubling. In response to her awareness she authored, "The Pet Negro System" (1943); "Negroes Without Self-Pity." (1943); "My Most Humiliating Jim Crow Experience" (1944); "Crazy for this Democracy" (1945); "I Saw Negro Votes Peddled" (1950); "What White Publishers Won't Prin" (1950); and, "A Negro Voter Sizes Up Taft (1951)." Most of those essays were viewed in the same light as much of her fiction by the critical community, but with a definite edge of anger that would show itself in the absence of support she would later need in a legal matter. These pieces were thought to be evidence of misdirected female fantasy and a lack of political savvy. Privately, there were personal affronts and expressions of indignation—the anger, she would learn, engendered the need for revenge, aimed at silencing.

Sadly . . . ultimately, she accepted the reality of the insufficiency of her characterizations of rural Black life in its simplicity and beauty to cause a change in the perception of others in either the Black or White world. Nonetheless, the lives, language, and philosophical perspectives of the communities that she had loved and learned from were set upon the world stage. For most, rural southern Blacks would remain, irretrievably, "backward." The "primitive" nature of her work was, after all, the attraction her writing held among White philanthropists in the early years in Harlem.

For more than twenty years she was quite convinced that fundamental social change was achievable. She had learned to smile at the appropriate time in the White world and to feign an impenetrable veneer, in many instances, when racism was open and damaging to her. She was also at odds with the way that Whites viewed Blacks as an amorphous group, all lumped into a single category of disposable, sub-humans. While they drew clear class and other distinctions among themselves, they could not stretch to imagine individuality among Blacks. In other words, ours was an uncomplicated existence—a singularly flat surface of sameness.

Did she really desire recognition as a writer who just happened to be Black, or was her literary identity linked, inseparably, to her Blackness? With the incipient personal transcendence came greater clarity that included the answer to this question. The two questions, obviously not binary opposites but obverse sides of the same coin, merged to assume a third, composite one. How might she achieve wholeness—what were her chances if she would be required to displace one part of herself in the "Other's" favor? Further, she was aware of "difference" among Blacks, based on her own experiences in both the North and South. Not only was there difference among individuals occupying the same general space, but there were regional distinctions. Blacks exhibited all of the particularities that are part and parcel of all ethnic group behavior.

Furthermore, Blacks in America, for instance, differ culturally from descendants of Africa, whose beliefs, values, and behavior she observed doing fieldwork in Haiti, Jamaica, Honduras, and

Nassau, in the Bahamas. An important aspect of her transcendence was a heightened social consciousness, and a new inner poetics that was related to coming to terms with this particular dimension of her inner life that, over a long period, had seesawed up and down—on one end, the primacy of race, the other, the efficacy of gender.

Along with Zora's consciousness and her transcendence, there were many bouts of illness, distress, and the grim financial outlook that had followed her throughout her life as a writer, but she was particularly impoverished during the 1950s and 1960s. The nagging abdominal distress increased in severity. She learned through the strife that if one manages to survive, illness has a way of settling the mind, redirecting, and strengthening the spirit. Close brushes with death also encourage forthrightness and honesty. She felt, therefore, that she should no longer guard her political opinions—to the extent that she ever had done so. Prior to this period of emergent revelation, she addressed the politics of American life through fiction and folklore—avoiding direct race-related statements.

Her writing also held up concepts of beauty, touched the despair of the aged, and, in its sweep, the multidimensional nature of life in southern Black communities. All of these life conditions existed in abundance in characters' lives and personalities and in the cultural spaces represented by quasi- fictionalized characters. Rural folk, she hoped to show, especially in her folklore collections, are insightful, resourceful, and philosophically and politically astute, despite their creolized, descriptive language of expression. Further, embedded in their language is a treasure trove of wit and wisdom, a lyrical pathos and ironic humor often inaccessible to outsiders' ears.

The sustained abdominal pain that she had for so long lived with nudged her toward those more openly politically charged essays noted earlier. Simultaneously she realized that her social world was decreasing in importance—parties and other gala events were no longer alluring. She had begun to favor quiet reflection above these things. The practice of introspection had become very much a part of her way of life. There were extended periods when she saw no one, neither friends nor family. She realized the difference between her mental state and that ghoulish figure that had engulfed her after her mother's death. Now, she was

not really depressed. There simply was a heightened awareness
. . . an inner awareness of herself and the world. This was very
different from other ways that she had known herself. This was a
time of physical infirmity, yet of healing. Now she healed from
the realization of years of fear and uncertainty, from acknowledgment of loss, and from unfulfilling and intransigent relationships. The formidable challenge was to move herself beyond the
realization that her associates had been rather limited at the level
of human interaction. She had learned, painfully, to accept life's
vicissitiudes across the years. She believed that once human limits were acknowledged, she would grow beyond time, beyond
the physical beginning and end of things.

Nyazema breathes, sings re/memberings . . . .

Full Moon: "Things Suffered, Things Enjoyed, Things Done and Undone"

She sent Isis to bed early that Thursday night but she herself lay awake
regarding the spider. She thought that she had not slept a moment, but
when in the morning Isis brought the wash basin and the tooth brush,
Lucy noted that the spider was lower and she had not seen it move.
Zora Neale Hurston, *Jonah's Gourd Vine*

[Haiti. I'm reading Haiti, writing, and thinking Haiti. The energy of
the words. . . . The power of the African ancestral spirit world—the
Fon-Kongo Cosmogram and Ve Ve]. Haiti. . . . No, there's no place
quite like Haiti for the way the culture merges pre-colonial African
cosmology with Black New World consciousness and our existence,
our physical existence in the West. It seems to me that Haiti
. . . your work there uncovered a spirituality and philosophical system
that deeply affected you. From my research and reading and fom all
that I understand, the turning inward which you began to feel in the
late 1940s is customary for a woman approaching her middle years.
Apparently, these years can frighten and alarm her. They can make
life difficult for many of us, but especially so when a woman's hopes
and dreams remain unfulfilled, her aspirations never brought to blos-
som. Similarly, the woman who looks back more than halfway down
the road of life's drama and discovers, belatedly, that she has no plans
at all, often recoils, and is pained by this revelation. I am not suggesting that either of us ought to consider your life in any way one of
tragedy, least of all, professionally, in the light of your productivity—
the fiction, folklore, and ethnographic writing. If there is tragedy, it is
that the writing was achieved at great personal cost. I'm referring to
the inordinate scrutiny and lifestyle critique that you sustained. Indeed, more than a half-century after the publication of *Their Eyes*,

the work is highly regarded by many critics, and the accolades that you might have missed, are now manifold. There remain a few critics, of course, who disavow *Their Eyes,* and others of your novels, as indicative of your unusual insight and sheer talent. That sentiment is not a reflection of the critical majority. Your fiction now appears on reading lists across humanities courses in most colleges and universities in America and it is the subject of papers at professional meetings and conferences nationwide.

I believe that you came to grips with the anger you felt as an artist who had scant financial resources in what I would call the latter stages of "transcendence." If during "transcendence" an entirely new set of disruptive, volcanic incidents had not befallen you (incidents to which I will later return), I believe that we all would likely have seen a metamorphosed Zora Neale Hurston.

Some of the current literature on the anthropology of women that I know of, written during the course of the last decade-and-a-half, emphasizes various psychological and physiological changes that women experience as they move toward the middle and mature years of life. In fact I have maintained an interest in cross-cultural studies of aging and aged women. Just as I completed requirements for the Master of Arts degree, nearly two decades ago, I was quite interested in research on women and gerontology and sought a research assistantship with a well known and respected scholar in the field. I had hoped to become involved in learning much more about this topic in a study of women and aging that, I had heard, she was soon to launch.

Women who are approaching their middle years, frequently evidence a lack of emotional accessibility and a tendency towards deep introspection. I use the term "mature women," to refer to those who are in, or approaching, menopause. Typically, during a self-reassessment, the woman devises an internal apparatus to cope with and to confront the reality of aging, intrinsic to the female human experience. Particular concern is given to menopause at this time, and she considers the sociological implications of the physical changes that she will experience. The probable extent of your engagement in this form of introspection has not yet been discussed in any of the existing literature of which I am aware. What memories do you hold of this type of experience? Others have noted a period when you appeared to isolate yourself and became less "accessible" than ever before. The obvious inclination toward aloneness that you showed during this period was dramatically clear and, I believe, misread by some of your associates before and after the morals charge was placed against you in 1948 in New York. I am convinced that denigrating calamity was the precipitating event before the full onset of your chronic illness, an illness that would, soon, increase in its severity.

The experience of arrest, alone, would be sufficient to shake almost anyone, but to have been falsely charged, according to the outcome of the case, with molesting a ten-year-old boy, had to have been the mortal psychic wound. Even though six months later the charge was dismissed by the Manhattan Office of the District Attorney, the damage to your reputation and personal dignitiy was irreparable. For me, a review of your comments following the arrest makes clear the devastation and indelibility of that episode.

I digress briefly. . . . When the morals scandal was first raised with me by an associate, I bristled, shocked. They were curious to know whether I really believed in your innocence. What did I think about it all? I pondered. The time was the late 1970s. I was, by that time, a Hurston zealot, although not yet a researcher, and was totally unaware that a morals charge was ever placed against you. But, here, I confess. Hearing of the charge, I was both startled and embarrassed. I believe that I was also shaken and frightened because I was not yet grounded sufficiently in the details of your life—not informed enough. . . . I was not . . . I could not wage a strong argument on your behalf. Nor did I know whether a *defense* was in keeping with so-called "facts." Why did I not trust my intuition? I cannot say—I wish that I could, but I cannot. I believed that I feared for you and myself. One Black woman already victimized, the other, a potential victim. What I was certain of was that you gave the world an invaluable, voluminous body of literature that represented a particular aspect of rural, southern Black life and culture, and much more. Your work enabled contemporary Black women writers to productivity.

My own ignorance caused me embarrassment when the morals charge was brought to my attention. Those words I heard, "child molestation," have a nasty ring. The warning: "You'd better be careful of the kinds of people you choose to study and admire. Child molesters should be prosecuted." These words resounded loudly, and repeated themselves within my mind. I agreed with them. More than anything, then, I wanted to know the story of your dishonor and your tragedy. My research effort assumed greater depth and inspired focus. Ultimately, I learned, once again, how dangerous and culpable we are in a racialized, gender-biased society.

At another level, my research on and writing about your life brought with it a new understanding of the politics of Black womanhood in the context of a society and world that continue to resist acceptance of our full humanity. While some have suggested that you were "distant" and "strange" before the morals charge, my research suggests that the *change* that others observed in you was related not to an inclination toward sexual encounters with adolescent males, but rather the interior life of a woman of your age. I add to these the consistent financial stress and quasi-social isolation that you experienced over four decades, and come up with an image of a middle-aged woman who is ill, exasperated, exhausted, and hunkering down, looking towards old age, and its myriad uncertainties. No doubt, you saw the writing on the wall.

I want to return . . . say more about your move inward, the introspection, and self-reassessment of the mid-1940s. What of the need to come to terms with certain aspects of your life such as childlessness—for you, the negation of motherhood. Was "bareness" a physiological insufficiency, or a conscious decision that you made, for whatever reason, for many are possible. One rationale might be consolidation of your energy for research and writing and the mobility and freedom of movement that you so valued. For we know that for the woman who *chooses* childlessness, eschews motherhood, and later regrets that decision; mid-life stock-taking can be traumatic. "Mother," and "nurturer" are roles, historically, assigned to Black women and, in the past, have been major qualifiers to achieving the status of "womanhood." In Black cultures, worldwide, frequently women without children suffer overt and subtle punishments, either at their own hand, or the hand of society, for transgressing *the* normative female role. And, I am certain, many women believe themselves to have violated their *natural* role if they desire motherhood and have not borne a child.

Some relevant literature suggests, further, that one might experience maladjusted middle- and old-age if the "motherhood" issue is not internally resolved. Women must successfully separate the issues of self-worth from biological motherhood. Many suffer great pressure, often a result of a particular cultural value that views motherhood efficaciously while allowing significant abuses against women. Just as a majority of women are biologically capable of childbearing, I view them as equally biologically suited to engage in intellectual challenges, social, and political leadership, and, say, the rigors of mathematics and science. These, too, are woman's "natural" domain.

For all outward appearances, the "motherhood" issue was settled with your commitment to a life of writing, for you were not an every-now-and-again writer. A steady stream of fiction, folklore, and ethnography poured forth from you. The high level of your productivity suggests that, for you, culture *reproduced* as text, was a representation of the "self," that you were, and filled the space in your life that children do for some. To push this notion further, one might argue that contemporary Black women writers are your progeny.

I also want to say something about the emphasis placed on youth and beauty throughout the West. That is, we are taught to strive toward the perpetuation of both into eternity. The yearning for youth and its binary opposite, a lack of appreciation and regard for the wisdom that most often accompanies aging, is not a worldwide phenomenon. A frenetic agitation attends many women's acknowledgment of the process of aging. In the West, there is a sociological gender imbalance that advantages males, in that the aging male is not the recipient of the same social pressure to continue appearing youthful as is true for women. How did these, or similar concerns, affect your life? A large body of literature exists now that focuses on women's "mid-life crisis," or "middle-age." The consensus of opinion seems to be that "the crisis" is something that we should all certainly expect to confront to a greater or lesser degree, sooner or later as a part of aging. Failure to grapple with the "crisis," we are warned, suggests that one is caught in a developmental quagmire that could produce serious consequences if left unattended. In 1948, your detractors attempted to create the image of you as a quirky, "love-starved" woman, one devoid of a moral conscience, and lacking internal discipline. Because that image of you was promulgated by some individuals whom you had angered, the charge of illicit sexual conduct with a young mentally retarded male apparently seemed believable to some.

Going right to the heart of the crisis, I know that the charge against you brought on thoughts of your demise—even your death. The prospect of death . . . one's attitude toward death is decidedly personal. It is the great "bogey" of middle-age, one might say, that begins with the realization of the existence of an infinitesimal unit in time, after which one must confront the great unknown, the abyss. I am aware of your consciousness of death because the sermons that you record in *Gourd Vine* speak of it (76, 151). The research that you conducted in Haiti, and Jamaica, and reported in *Tell My Horse*, plumb the depths of human time, and our dissolution (376). Death is the supreme fear of much of the Western world. It is a fear that is deeply rooted in the dominant cultures of Europe and the New World. Yet, some of your experiences in voudun (voodoo), and the occult practices that you observed and participated in in Haiti, Jamaica, and New Orleans, may have suggested the appropriateness of an alternative attitude towards death, one not in keeping with mainstream Western culture and cosmology.

Boldly *independent* is, I believe, an appropriate description of your temperament in the early years of the era of the New Negro. You cautioned the wind, tempted fate—and, yes, even courted death. I say with certainty that you held scant regard for the life of safety and low-risk, "atypical" of most of your female contemporaries. Of course, there were other women who led unsheltered lives, but they were, by no means, a majority. How many contemporary women would, say, buy a houseboat and live on a waterway with alligators for several years? How many of us would submit to an initiation into voudoun for the sake of participant observation or science? Few, I would argue. Fortunately, your sojourns into the dangerous and unknown seem to have brought you no immediate or obvious harm.

My friend, I think we ought to face facts. Not very much that was or could be thought to have been "good," or "fortuitous" occurred in your life following that morals scandal, the dread-filled morals charge. The whole mess was quite ugly and, obviously, debilitating. The entire encounter appears to have been utterly demoralizing. For you, the incredulity—such a terrible thing—appearing from out of nowhere. The numbness, first, and then the reality. Not only was the charge one that would cause more anguish than you had ever dreamed possible, but it was leveled at a most inopportune time—that of your inward-turning, reassessment, and nascent renewal. Had "the scandal" not subverted your evolution, the world might have witnessed a new Zora. By "new" I simply intend to suggest a blending, or merging of old and new spirits.

The transcendence seems to have begun three to four years prior to the morals charge—the dreadful finger of blood pointed toward you. This was the bomb—an attack sustained without allies, without . . . without the comfort of deep and abiding friendships. A cruel twist of fate. Yes, you were acquitted. But was an acquittal sufficient to repair a broken heart and a maimed spirit? These questions rise and fall, ebb and flood my thoughts like ocean waves, they rise and fall.

Existing evidence shows that some of the most cynical criticisms of you were offered by journalists who appeared to seek nothing more than a sensation—a story. A story similar to the one reported in the Black news organ, *New York Age* in October 1948, which read: "Noted Novelist Denies She Abused 10-Year Old Boy: Zora Neale Hurston Released on Bail." The *Afro-American*, another Black newspaper, in Baltimore, released a more sensationalized account of your trouble, using a provocative quote from your novel, *Seraph*: "I'm just as hungry as a dog for a knowing and doing love."

Who would not have been heartbroken. My study of your life suggests that because of the morals charge, you resolved to die. And, slowly by degrees, you surrendered, if not invited death to knock at your door. The life that was once filled with meaning and vigor was no more. There was not a resurgence of your energy following the court's dismissal of the charges against you. There was only accelerated deterioration and decline. Seemingly, you were stressed to excess, and your body and spirit weakened. In photographs taken around that time, you appear to be something of a caricature of the former Zora. You appear heavy, fleshy, and sometimes even untidy. This image is so distant from the stylish, self-guided woman who was once so filled with laughter and told funny stories.

By this time, the Harlem *literati* had long since dispersed . . . and who could predict what might have been their collective response to your despair? Who is to say that the charge against you was not related to alleged incidents of "misconduct" from an earlier period? Stated differently, how piercing and unnerving, for some, was your outspokenness on social and political issues? Convinced as I am that there was a direct relationship between certain of your publications such as "The Rise of the Begging Joints" (1945), in which you critique inferior Black colleges, and the morals charge, between your satirical essay, "Crazy for This Democracy" (1945), and the morals charge, only strong evidence could otherwise sway me. Moreover, your condemnation of the U.S. is apparent in these essays for having denied freedom to Blacks at home. Such published, strong opinion was, I believe, seditiously consequential for the maintenance of relationships between you and the influential people who might, otherwise, have come to your aid. In short, I am suggesting the presence of a conspiracy to silence an opinionated, rather fearless Black woman. For after all, society, generally, and our families and friends, particularly, insist on our enduring nurturance and sacrifice. The problem, therefore, it seems to me, is that your life defied and defiled historical myths and images of Black women—"nanny," "nurturer," "Mother Earth," and the like.

Rare and atypical are descriptives such as "writer," "scholar," "social architect," or "thinker." In my analysis, the scandal became the useful means to achieve your silence, a means to an end. This was the high price you paid for daring to speak and write.

Those of us who wish to speak and write, contemporarily, sometimes find ourselves alienated and distanced from loved ones. Friendship and family require time and sustenance—long talks and reminiscing. Seldom is there the luxury of time for the writer to "explore" and "share," for time and solitude are the twin demands of the craft of writing. How often have Black women spoken and written about feelings of isolation and alienation? Aloneness is necessary to productivity but differs from the sort of loneliness that you confronted in 1948. Besides, writing women are deemed a threat to male dominance. Black women face double jeopardy—the twin assassins that are race and gender. When you became the victim of powerful detractors and were labeled, "child molester," the Black community offered you neither support nor defense. They became more your critics and reviled you.

The attempts at writing continued following the scandal. You also took a job as a maid, slowly moving away from public view, almost completely, away from an environment that seemed almost to celebrate your tragedy. I recall that you returned to the South, always the place of your healing. Never again . . . never, following the scandal would you to live in New York City.

There was also irony in all of this. The glaring irony—the irony is the obvious: In the closing pages of your most widely read novel, *Their Eyes*, Janie Mae stands trial on a murder charge. She is accused of murdering the man whose love she fought for, and who so dearly loved her. Janie, too, is acquitted, found innocent of the charge and released. And although she reclaims her freedom, the Black and White communities have come to court to judge her.

Like you, Janie was a woman alone—she was alone and judged. Janie's great fear was not death, her fear was that others, the community, would not understand the depth of her love for the man she was forced to kill in self-defense. Their failure to understand and believe her motive was a fate far worse than the murder charge. Free, then, to return to her community, Janie appears stronger than ever before, for she has found deeper spiritual insouciance emerging from her day in court.

Considering the events that were to soon occur in your life, the morals scandal in New York foretold the incipient depletion of your physical and mental energies, the consummate requirements for the craft of writing.

Nyazemaaaa. Ride the sound of my voice,
Ride the breath of the wind . . . .

A Spirit Departing

Nyazema. . . . The name, the sound filled her with a kind of comfort, ease, that one could call completeness. The bridge . . . we cross the bridge now, and it is done. Sisters of the sky bridge. Looking back she can see her life now, the shadow of her life. The connections, the actions, and interactions. They are linked, bound in ways that were never before quite clear to her. No, not at all clear as she moved from day-to-day. It is difficult, in the midst of it all, to see the circles within circles that make a life. She might sit down, just now, just as she is, and sketch it all out, recognizing how one decision led to another. How precisely the days crossed over themselves, made a quick loop, and came right back to her again. Interesting . . . that the story of Janie Mae Crawford was born little more than a decade before that nightmarish "scandal." Yet, there are strong parallels between the morals charge against her and the villification of her fictional character, Janie Mae Crawford, following Tea Cake's death.

In the novel you recall that a hurricane strikes the Everglades, where Janie, Tea Cake, and some of their friends have gone. Everything, nearly everything on land is washed away, twisted and gnarled, destroyed in the hurricane's wake. Death rides the high winds, and the rising water. Realizing that it is impossible to stay where they are Janie and Tea Cake move out and attempt to reach Palm Beach and safety. If they can reach the bridge, they reason, there is hope of saving their lives. Groping, stumbling, and crawling, they come upon a land elevation only to discover that Whites had made it there first and, consequently, there is no space for them. Janie and Tea Cake move on until they come to a landfill where Tea Cake, exhausted, falls asleep, having had to swim, carrying Janie, much of the way through angry, tumultuous waters. In Janie's effort to catch hold of a large piece of tar-paper roofing afloat on the water, that she plans to use as a cover for Tea Cake, she crawls to the edge of the landfill. The strong wind pushes her headlong into the raging water. Janie's screams for help awaken Tea Cake, who shouts instructions to her to grab hold of the tail of a cow drifting swiftly toward her. Struggling to catch the animal's tail, Janie's eyes fall on an apparition. There, riding nervously on the cow's back, she sees a large, yellow dog, his mouth frothing. The cow comes closer to Janie, the dog edges toward the cow's hind parts, poised to attack her. Tea Cake, now in the water, swims hard to reach them. He wrestles the rabid dog and manages to stab him to death. In the fray, the mad dog bites Tea Cake, once, high on the cheek.

Shortly after their brush with death Janie and Tea Cake finally reach land and safety. Janie observes, at once, that Tea Cake's behavior is suddenly frightening and erratic. He suffers fits of rage and anger, which become longer, and has frequent bouts of absolute madness and dissociation. Viewing Janie through his distorted vision, brought on by the ravages of fever, Janie has become the enemy—the enemy who must be destroyed. Surreptitiously, Janie calls a doctor, who comes to treat Tea Cake and leaves medicine. He also instructs Janie to sleep apart from him until the medicine takes effect and Tea Cake shows improvement. In his delirium, Tea Cake argues that the choice to sleep with him, or on a floor pallet, is Janie's. Because of his delirium, he is unable to discriminate between the machinations brought on by fever and delirium from the rabid dog's bite, and his rage and anger towards Janie. He imagines that she no longer loves and desires him, and the floor pallet that the doctor instructed Janie to sleep on is, for Tea Cake, evidence of her rejection and scorn.

The "listener" is aware of Tea Cake's marksmanship and knows that he also taught Janie to use a gun. Tea Cake loves guns and always keeps one close. In these very tense and halting moments, Janie appreciates the depth and seriousness of her situation. Fever laden, Tea Cake stumbles to the outhouse, which allows Janie time to hide a shell in her apron pocket, grab the shot gun from behind the bed, and cock it. She also manipulates the three shells in Tea Cake's gun so that he must fire three times before a bullet will reach the chamber. Tea Cake has exerted great effort traveling to and from the outhouse, and falls into a deep sleep immediately after he returns.

Even more enraged when he awakens, Tea Cake, again, confronts Janie and accuses her of rejection. Now in the supreme moment of his madness, Tea Cake levels the gun, aiming at Janie's breast. She pleads with him to put the gun down and return to bed. Crazed, Tea Cake, instead, fires twice and misses. His third shot is the shadow of Janie's discharge of the single shot gun shell. Tea Cake falls forward and slumps into her arms.

Zora rethinks Janie's trauma, her ordeal, and sees her character's life as a dramatic harbinger of events that would come in her own. She diverges for a moment. . . . The denouement of Janie's story also echoes our lives and mirrors the lives of Black people in America. The "mad dog" biting Tea Cake? A metaphor, a representation of racial strife? The unreasoned illness that destroys, that cannot accept responsibility, and blinds both victim and victimizer?

During the course of her life Zora traveled to several islands and countries with large Black settlements that are, in most instances, the consequence of earlier enslaved communities. Various forms of Black rage existed in these communities. This rage and anger are the accumulation of pain and distress from centuries of dehumanizing treatment of Blacks by Whites. Blacks, themselves, have also internalized racist notions about themselves that assume the form of self-hatred that shows itself in myriad forms of communal violence and disorder. She was aware that others, many others before her had expressed similar thoughts, yet she reiterated their thoughts—the pressure of injustice often became intolerable, the rage displaced, and victims of the combustive energy were human sacrifices on the altar of despair. Nothing more than an attack on a mirror image of oneself.

Janie Mae Crawford's story has multiple meanings, but central to it is the representation of aspects of Black life as experienced through the progenitive force of a Black woman who seeks wholeness and fulfillment in the face of many obstacles. Prior to meeting Tea Cake, Janie was treated as an object by the men she married. Tea Cake, her true love, is driven mad by the bite of an angry yellow dog. One dimension of this character is the "Black community"—the locus of a collectivized, internal anger, and volatile rage. The proverbial ticking time-bomb. All too often violence in the Black community is an expression of rage created outside of the communal space but finds expression inside in the form of explosive behaviors—"kill or be killed."

Janie's options are obviously narrowed by Tea Cake's madness: commit virtual suicide, or take the life of the beloved. Some critics have argued that Janie should not have killed Tea Cake. What are her choices? Self-destruction or murder in self-defense? Tough choices. Nevertheless the challenge remains for the "listeners" contemplation, for if the novel's denouement represents the Black community—the mad dog's bite—what then? We know that internalized racism disrupts Black life, creates adversarial relationships that take the form of inter- and intra-community distancing, self-loathing, and feelings of alienation. Zora wanted to depict some of these attitudes and used Ms. Turner and the "porch sitters" as stand-ins for the larger Black social world.

Going back again now, Janie's horrific experience—being faced with the two choices: her life or Tea Cake's resonates with Zora's morals charge "scandal." This was her "mad dog," intruding in her life several years after the publication of *Their Eyes*. She faced her nightmare alone. With the death of Tea Cake, Janie faces the loss of a long sought after relationship, one of deep value. She also fights, heroically, the memory of her grandmother's well intentioned advice and an inviolate community. Painfully lost to Zora in the scandal, the nightmare, was a sense of faith in humanity and, especially, Black humanity. This was a loss of faith that made itself over and became an engulfing sadness, bitterness, and rancor toward her people. That searing pain and gross disappointment were never to fade. *Their Eyes* depicts Blacks and Whites turning out to see, and to witness Janie's trial. She becomes the spectacle: a Black woman on trial accused of murdering her young lover.

In her own life, she witnessed a turning away of her associates to her ordeal. The Black community left a void in the space where her spirit, and essence once nested. The morals charge (especially, the allegation of "child abuse"), and her "porch sitters'" reaction bore right through her heart, like a bullet, bruising and tearing away flesh. She would never heal from the distress and emotional pain created by the vicious attacks from the press and beyond. In the novel, Janie Mae is acquitted at the trial's end. She is also lifted above community scorn by the power of her own words in the recapitulation of the events of her life for Pheoby.

When the community criticizes Janie, Pheoby mediates and buffers their negative comments. The story leaves the "listener" with the impression that Janie survived. Her friendship with Pheoby and cherished memories of life with Tea Cake are powerful enough to offset her suffering. Pheoby experiences an enhanced sense of herself as a result of Janie's "storytelling" incantations—her words, magically, create a new woman in Pheoby.

Janie, too, is a mature woman. She has grown not only from the pleasures she holds inside, but also because of the pain and life challenges she faced. Although fate was unkind, Janie realized her heart's desire in the form of control over her life, rather than being controlled, and the consummated ideal love that she so longed for. Her search for wholeness is complete.

As Zora thinks of wholeness, she recalls the most powerful of all goddesses—the Great Goddess, Isis of Egypt. Isis has many manifestations: among them is Nut, goddess of the night sky. She is also the goddess Hathor, the sacred cow, wearing the sun disk between her horns. Most importantly, it is Isis who reconnects the dismembered body of the god Osiris, making him whole after his dismemberment. Janie performs similar "word-magic," empowering and making Pheoby whole. Janie's "word-magic" also serves the dual purpose of reconnecting the disparate parts of her own psyche—she heals and is healed by their power. Zora was about fifty years old when she confronted the morals charge, as compared to Janie who, in the novel, was a woman in her late forties at the time of Tea Cake's death. Perhaps Janie's travail was also more than coincidental.

The advent of her middle-years had a definite impact on her outlook on life, as she began to withdraw from the social scene in New York. She believed that middle-age, and to a lesser extent the "mature years," are often traumatic for women in our society. Zora closely scrutinized the physical changes in her body and was frustrated to realize that time was pressing on, and the open road lay before her. There seemed to be a greater ease coming to terms with the physical aspects of aging than with the sociological ones. By "sociological" she meant the way aging women are often treated as outcasts or throwaways. She had come to terms with the physical dimensions of aging by the time of her emergence from self-imposed isolation. It was really a period of deep reflection and refocusing.

Neither she nor others perceived the slow metamorphosis that would lead to "transcendence." She later sensed the pieces coming together within her, slowly coming together, each searching for its place. It is true that very little, if anything, is written about that phase of her life, the not so obvious part. She agreed that women are encouraged throughout their lives to fear change—particularly the loss of youth and external beauty. Because they learn to embrace this fear early in life, aging is thought of with disdain. It is not regarded as a special phase in the life cycle, especially for women. Women are enculturated to "preserve" themselves for as long as possible and by any means necessary. Not a very healthy attitude.

She mused over her choices, those concerning marriage and childlessness. Were she a contemporary woman, no doubt the question whether or not to have a child might have been a separate one from that of whether to marry. No doubt, many women today *choose* single parenthood. In her lifetime the decision to parent as a single woman would have seemed the nearest mental state to madness—although it sometimes happened. Then, too, the 1920s and 1930s were years not so far removed from the turn of the century.

It is a peculiar and strange thing that a woman who chooses childlessness is often thought to be "odd" or "weird." When one considers that motherhood was, once, a woman's only "natural" role, then, such an attitude is better understood. One might rightly or wrongly surmise the one reason she might have regretted not bearing a child is that she missed sharing the precious gift of love in the way she felt loved by her mother. But she never brooded over motherhood, that is, the absence of it. Childlessness never made a big difference in how she felt about herself as a woman. Of that, she was confident. But in the time of her retrospection, and self-assessment, she thought deeply about all aspects of her life, up to then, up to the time of her inward turning.

The circles of life can confound as life unfolds in the way it often does—at a quite rapid pace. Fortunately, she formed, early, the habit of acknowledging her inner voice, a long time before she felt a pressing need for interiority. Her tendency toward introspection was related to the considerable time that she spent alone, as a child and, later, in womanhood, contemplating and puzzling over how to make her life a successful venture, without sustained emotional support and financial means. There really was nowhere to turn, other than within to allay these questions.

· Was she slowing down, and her body changing? Yes. So, too, were her interests shaping themselves differently. She required more time alone and was comfortable that way—alone with herself. Reluctantly, she acknowledged an unyielding pride. There she was, a woman who never wished to appear weak, out of control, or in need of emotional support. There is no doubt that she was in constant need of financial resources, but so were her peers. Yes, that need could be acknowledged, spoken aloud, because nearly everyone, all of her associates, the Harlem writers, lived with a similar predicament. But Zora felt a need to prove certain points, especially that she could make it on her own, against the odds. Admittedly, pride got her into trouble more than once in life. Yet, had she to do it all again, her hunch is that she would play it nearly the same way. Adjustments? Perhaps, but not very many.

Adjustments, such as what, you ask? Well . . . she would try to map out a way to make the big love encounter work! She believed that she would give a little more. She thought, mulling it over, maybe she was just not resourceful enough confronting the "man or the work" options. Yet this was the dilemma, the kind of all or nothing existence a "professional" woman had to confront in that era—this was the prevailing social mandate. Again and again, she used to ask herself, what would have been different had she been more patient with him, waited a while for the idea of her work to settle on him. She also considered that maybe she was too self-absorbed. And, might they have come to a more reasonable arrangement than she going her way, and he going his? Clearly, he, too, would have had to make certain attitudinal adjustments. She is not sure that he could have. Zora recounted the passion and excitement of their time together. Haltingly, she moved her thoughts toward the question whether her life would have been more fulfilled with than without him. These questions remained unsatisfactorily answered. She knows only that life and writing remained a single undifferentiated thought. She poured over all of this and more and felt good about it, rather enjoying a sense of acceptance and internal peace. When contemplation ended, there seemed to be a return of tranquility, brief though it would be, and inner harmony. And then it all happened, her entire world ruptured—caved in. The horror of the morals charge, the nightmare, and her life.

The scandal hit like an ill-wind from the Arctic, it came right out of nowhere, like the Everglade hurricane in the novel. She was totally unprepared for such a turn of events. A bolt of lightening that numbs to the point of causing one to stagger and stumble. All sensibilities were deadened by the power of shock and surprise—something that strikes in the darkness. She could hear, see, and speak . . . communicate, but seemingly from another world. The numbness was psychic insulation, the only protection that she had against the macabre accusation until she could gather the strewn parts of herself. Bearing the full impact of such an ambush is sufficient to sink one to the depths of hell and damnation. Before the loss of feeling sets in the "victim" of unreality takes in just enough of the pain to beg to die from its presence. Zora's mind was bombarded by dull and sharp plunderous blows. She was the vanquished. The demons had come to carve out her heart and take her life. At the threshold of death from pain she knew that her life was at stake, and the pitch darkness of her soul, surely, was death. She called on her mother's spirit, prayed, and propitiated the ancient goddesses of Africa. She summoned the spirit cult of her initiation and prayed for intercession. So vexed was her soul that she psychically shook the grave markers of all the ancestral cults known to her, imploring them to rescue her from the dragon that ate at her bones.

A White man, a lawyer, finally aided her. He befriended her. She, like Janie, had a day in court. Janie defended herself against a charge of murder, Zora against child sexual abuse. You might think of it this way: the White male lawyer symbolizes the only real power in America, other than money. She, a Black woman, represents the opposite end of the power spectrum. And so there she was Black, female, and quite poor. And, he, White, male, and financially comfortable. He was all, she, nothing. Certainly, she was grateful that he was there, yet it was strange. Somehow his strength seemed predicated on her weakness, even relied on her for its existence.

Another way of looking at the situation is to see her as a perpetually marginal person, and by the time the scandal hit, she lived in a triple bind, as opposed to the double bind of racism and sexism. There was, then, the added dimension of age. And, who, other than a benevolent White man, would be interested in "saving" a Black woman approaching fifty years of age? Yes, she knows that a fifty-year-old woman can be vital, can be beautiful, but a general view of an aging woman tends to negate either prospect. Some might have mused that to the White man Zora symbolized the powerlessness of all Black people and he felt stronger than usual because he was far beyond the circle of her powerlessness. She was no threat to his place in the universe, and he could, therefore, afford to save her from the wolves, many of whom were Black wolves.

The embarrassment and uncertainty—knowing you admired and respected a public person who was centrally implicated in a child abuse scandal would cause her sadness. You are quite right: even knowing the truth was not sufficient to right a wrong situation. She would not be shocked to know that eyebrows still rise whenever someone, who has not heard of the incident, hears about it the first time. Her new sense of self, the woman that she strove to bring into existence was violated and diminished nearly to the point of oblivion by the trauma. Zora wondered why society seemed to want her life and was incredulous. The whole thing was so far-fetched. Days and nights were endless, and merged in a most unusual way—sometimes a single night lived on for three or four days. She was confused, unsure, mauled, and bitten by a "mad, rabid dog." Inside herself she screamed in a high pitch, singing the saddest, sorrowful song. A song of death. She survived only with a part of herself alive.

Zora always thought rather philosophically about life, and in the weeks immediately following the scandal, reflection would help her to appreciate the usefulness of her outlook. She believed that she could overcome most obstacles, under two conditions: understanding a given situation and commitment to work hard to change or to maintain her position, if that became necessary. It was this outlook that finally aided her in moving toward a psychological center—recovering some of life's orderliness. She also felt the need to reaffirm many of her past choices. The work was hard but, oddly, enjoyable. Zora sought after her old enthusiasm for life but often found it difficult to rise in the morning with positive thoughts and a hopeful outlook. Before regaining her equilibrium, she was convinced that some similarly awful experience would engulf her again, take over, and misdirect her life. And so the road back to herself was long and arduous. At the deepest level she had lost interest in life, in the world around her. Everything appeared to be as dead as she felt inside. Finally, her inner voice began to whisper some of the old familiar phrases, those that revitalized her in trials past.

Zora pondered how she kept herself alive after her mother's death—recalled all that she left her. The instructions . . . yes, and her mother's wisdom about life reverberated from the depth of her being. Slowly, her thoughts turned to the good years and to her work. The novels, stories of the rural folk, her travels, and the lusty excitement of new places. Feelings of melancholy attached themselves to her books. She was financially unsuccessful, but reflections of a way of life that she strongly desired and from which she felt some success emerged. It was good to know that she had formed those words . . . they became the books. And a book takes on a life of its own, beyond that of its progenitor.

Those old tales from home—just the thought of them strengthened her wounded spirit. They would be preserved for generations yet unborn. The mind and body are remarkable, she mused, and their power seemingly infinite. Convinced by personal knowledge of certain healing rituals, she reasoned that her will to live was rooted in a time beyond memory. Yet, she was aware of the great damage she had suffered from more recent events.

Zora was aware when things were happening within her body that signaled danger. Even though she may have appeared oblivious to certain changes, there had been danger signs of all kinds emanating from the inside out for quite a long time. Somehow, she was simply unable to heed them. Perhaps because she was driven to complete *Herod,* to bring it full circle, she thought that she could just continue working, and everything would, eventually, fall into place. *Herod* had lived inside of her since the early 1940s and was a growing internal presence pushing to freedom, seeking expression. Her prayer was to finish it—to complete the writing before it was too late. She was a woman, driven.

Although at the level of conscious thought Zora was keenly aware of the magnitude of her stresses, the physical, emotional, and financial, and her advancing years, she took on the *Herod* project with all that was left of her. What was left, it seems, was not equal to the task. She seemed not able to pull off the epic of her dreams. In 1955, the publishers were simply not interested. Zora had hoped that others would share her vision that was *Herod,* and now she was disappointed. Furthermore, she needed money, badly. But neither financial gain nor its prospect was the spur. Financial concerns pressed in on her mind because of the practical aspects of sustaining life (a knock at the door, an unfriendly voice demanding unpaid rent). Convinced as she was that uniform critical acclaim was just around the corner, she had,

habitually, stretched and pushed herself to write for long periods, to write often. Reflecting . . . she supposes that had *Herod*
been the work, the big one that she hoped for, the story might
have just forced itself right out of her, long before it had come. It
would have demanded time and space in her life

By the late 1950s Zora's energy was seriously ebbing to non-
existence. But sometimes staying alive seemed less important than
depriving herself of small satisfactions. The emotional often out-
distances the cognitive. If all one has is the thinnest edge of life,
that edge is often no more than the will to live. Yes, she wanted
to survive, longed for good health, yet she could see her physical
dissolution. She knew that real survival hinged on financial sustenance. She was even more aware of the way that it had eluded
her for so many years. The only way, she thought, that she might
come into security was by producing an attractive book that was
critically acclaimed and a popular success. She became desper-
ate. The harder she tried to ignore what was behind her, the more
she felt drawn to things past.

Forgetfulness. That was what she needed and wanted—to forget painful experiences of the past. She longed to turn out an
engaging work that would put her in a secure place. At the same
time she felt the presence of a creeping skepticism, too real to
ignore. She was skeptical that her epic would not be worthy of
print. The deeper the fear and reticence, the more strained and
disjointed was the writing. Most of all, she was drained, the energy washed out of her. This realization added to her already
burdened, wrecked body.

Zora moved to Eau Gallie, found comfort there, and stayed
about five years, from 1953 until 1958. Still not writing well, she
took on odd jobs, including a library clerkship at Patrick Air Force
Base. None of her employment situations would bring financial
security. She managed to complete a few articles for the *Pitts-
burgh Courier* and the *Saturday Evening Post*, but these were not
the kinds of projects that would boost her out of the red and
provide income sufficient to secure medical care and other life
necessities. For more than thirty years solvency had eluded her.
Now stability was not simply a desire, it was a real emergency.
She was tired, sick, disheartened, and, of course, broke. As much
as anything, she was panicky when the one thing she believed to
be her niche no longer appeared to work. More than that, she

depended on writing as a source of psychic comfort. The odd jobs were poor substitutes for writing, and, furthermore, they were strange and ill-fitted to her.

Repeatedly, she studied the drama of her life, and her life-long commitment to writing. Thirty years? No, longer. Forty. Then she wondered why had she had not considered other options, something more stable. Surely, she could have become proficient at . . . something other than writing. Again and again she reminded herself of her love of writing. Writing and life were one and the same. There was no remorse for that. Some of the toughest decisions of her life had been in deference to an internal mandate to write.

In this cul-de-sac now, Zora couldn't resist wondering why she was not more flexible and less caught up in a big dream, one that extended all the way from Eatonville, Florida, to New York City, and around the Caribbean. Whatever had made her believe that she could make a real life of writing, that she could support herself . . . ? She was approaching seventy years of age now and finding it impossible to put together an acceptable manuscript—one that a publisher would find acceptable? Yet, turning her situation upside down, inside out, and looking at it from every possible angle, she remained committed to her dream, even if it now failed her. Zora loved the craft and had given it most of her passion, and nearly all of her life.

She forced concentration on other things. Yes, she was a child of the natural world, one who was most comfortable near water, wooded areas, and a warm climate. Again, she sought refuge there. It occurred to her that she would feel better if she moved closer to nature. Perhaps, she would plant a vegetable garden! A flower patch? These things she did, and the results were good. With a bountiful crop, she healed a little inside. There was more internal calm and less frenetic pondering her circumstances. Once more she made a pact with herself never again to look back. The past was the past, and life is always a forward motion. Brooding, she was sure, would not change her reality, either of her physical condition, or the financial one. As for the abdominal pain and elevated blood pressure, they, too, seemed permanent. Damage to her arteries, she had learned, was significant, and her heart was strained both by body weight and the condition of her arteries. She realized the depth of her trouble, yet her mind was, strangely, clearer than at any time in the recent past. Even rejection of the *Herod* manuscript had not, permanently, rattled her. It was reasonable to have been upset by the rejection of such a long writing effort. But that was over. Had she become immune to anguish? She saved her small earnings from Patrick in Cocoa Beach.

There was another move, this time to Fort Pierce, Florida, where she began writing somewhat regularly for the *Fort Pierce Chronicle*. Because she was weak most of the time, newspaper articles were about all that she could manage in the way of regular writing. When energy allowed, she reworked the *Herod* manuscript. Were she to focus on her physical condition or financial situation, the reality of either was almost instantly overpowering.

Zora had responded so intensely to incidents over the past decade-and-a-half, that her body assumed a permanent state of decline, and she suffered the first stroke in 1959. The warnings were abundantly clear. The near total loss of energy was a signal that things were very bad. She was quite easily distracted. This vulnerability, she had reasoned, was responsible for her difficulty with the *Herod* manuscript. Remembering, at any time . . . the fertile years . . . opened the floodgates of her imagination, and hour after hour the waters flowed. She would break, return, and the waves of word images flooded all over again.

After the stroke, moving around became more difficult and labored. But she managed to put out a few pieces every now and then for the *Chronicle*. She was not depressed so much because of the stroke as she was, in a way, shocked that she was its victim. In a certain respect she must have thought herself invincible. It was kind of like the scandal, the horror in New York. Shock and disbelief. Most amazing was the sense of unreality that the stroke produced. How could so many things have gone wrong so quickly? Only a short time ago Zora had been fun-loving, energetic, hopeful, and spirited. And, yes, some had called her an audacious woman. There was no question that she traveled widely and wrote voraciously for many years. And then, suddenly, she was practically unable to perform even the most basic functions for herself. She suspected that most of the aged and seriously ill experience similar astonishment and disbelief. Helplessness, she was to learn, is profoundly demoralizing. Sickness and even death, were others' reality, but she had not considered either, until the first stroke. If she could have thought of herself in that way, the whole matter would have been far easier. But she could not, and she remained virtually incredulous to what was happening to her. Zora had become, essentially, helpless. She remembered her mother's failing health—her dearly, beloved mother, and she had thought that certainly she would be spared in the final hour. How wrong she had been then.

Because Zora was very poor, she became a county welfare case. She dug down deep into herself and looked for the truth, for this time, there was no escape, no way out. She fought depression and disillusionment, reminding herself again and again that self-pity is the most destructive of forces. Only occasionally did she win. It seemed that she grew increasingly weak with every passing day and fought to focus on what might be the outside miracle—a chance that she would experience moderate recovery. No matter how long and hard she wrestled the odds, there was no hope. Her thoughts turned, again, to the past. Where was everyone, all of those she had known over forty years ago? Pained at her own response, she was reminded that no great and lasting friendships had evolved. But there were meaningful associations, were there not? Where was the world that she once knew? Where, she wanted to know . . . was her life. A few strong bonds of friendship are easy, aren't they? Good times in Harlem with . . . ? Well, she pondered. They had all believed in that world then. They were sure that their mark would be made and that they would change things. Sure. They were sure of it. But where had the world gone? Was she not the same woman who had, confidently, embarked on a 1500-mile trip all the way from Florida to New York in a houseboat, what seemed just a few years ago. She had arrived victorious, proud, and unscathed. Was it not true that she once wrote a novel in seven weeks? No . . . that was not so long ago. Why, she thought . . . was she cursed? Her limbs . . . so weak, so weak that she could barely feel them. Hers, she was reminded, were the same hands that she used to write for days, tirelessly. . . . Where, she wondered, had the world gone? Saint Lucie County Welfare . . . no, she had not wanted to go.

Somehow, she managed to avoid the old "square-toed" one for several weeks out there. But it was a high-speed chase through the prisms of her often drifting mind. He was after her, and she managed, several times, to elude his clutches. She watched him. She watched him closely. It wasn't very long ago, she would dream. Where is everyone now? Each time "the old square-toed one" stirred from his big, old platform in the backyard, Zora out-smarted him. Perceptive. She was still perceptive and sensed his every move. And then late one evening while she was dreaming of a beautiful sunset on Lake Okechobee, nodding, and dozing just a bit, she missed old "square toes'" tiny motion. Quietly, ever so quietly, he climbed down the worn platform stairs, eased into her room catching her quite by surprise. Zora was startled but they neither exchanged harsh words nor struggled with one another. Finally, he made his manners, bowing, modestly. She nodded and acknowledged him. She remembered it all so clearly. The day was January 28, 1960, and he had won.

Works Consulted

Angrosino, Michael V. "Dub Poetry and West Indian Identity." *Anthropology and Literature*. Ed. Paul Benson. Urbana: U of Illinois P, 1993. 73–88.

Ani, Marimba. *Yurugu*. Trenton: Africa World, 1994.

Appadurai, Arjun. "The Heart of Whiteness." *Callaloo* 16.4 (Fall 1993): 796–807.

Armah, Ayi Kwei. *The Healers*. Nairobi, Kenya: East African Publishing House, 1978.

Ashley, Kathleen M. *Victor Turner and the Construction of Cultural Criticism: Between Literature and Anthropology*. Bloomington: Indiana UP, 1990.

Aunger, Robert. "On Ethnography: Storytelling or Science." *Current Anthropology* 36.1 (1995) 97–114.

Baer, Hans A. *The Black Spiritual Movement: A Religious Response to Racism*. Knoxville: U of Tennessee P, 1984.

Baker, Houston. *Modernism and the Harlem Renaissance*. Chicago: U of Chicago P, 1987.

Behangue, Gerard H. *Music and Black Ethnicity: The Caribbean and South America*. New Brunswick: Transaction, 1994.

Bell, Roseann, Bettye Parker, and Beverly Guy-Sheftall. *Sturdy Black Bridges: Visions of Black Women in Literature*. Garden City: Doubleday, 1979.

Boas, Franz. *Anthropology and Modern Life*. New York: W.W. Norton, 1962.

Bobo, Jacqueline. *Black Women as Cultural Readers*. New York: Columbia UP, 1995.

Boxwell, D. A. "'Sis Cat'" as Ethnographer: Self-Presentation and Self-Inscription in Zora Neale Hurston's *Mules and Men*. *African American Review* 26.4 (1992): 605–17.

Briffault, Robert. *The Mothers*. New York: Atheneum, 1977.

Brady, Ivan, ed. *Anthropological Poetics*. Savage: Rowman & Littlefield, 1991.

Bruner, Edward. "Introduction: The Ethnographic Self and the Personal Self." Ed. Paul Benson. Urbana: U of Illinois P, 1993.

Butler-Evans, Elliott. "Constructing and Narrativizing the Black Zone: Semiotic Strategies of Black Aesthetic Discourse." *Semiotics* 6.1 (1988/89): 19–35.

Campbell, Mavis C. *The Maroons of Jamaica, 1655–1796*. Trenton: Africa World P, Inc., 1990.

Cannon, Katie. *Black Womanist Ethics*. Atlanta: Scholars P, 1988.

Chesnut, Charles W. *The Conjure Woman*. 1899. Reprint. Darby, Pennsylvania: Arden Library, 1978.

Christian, Barbara. *Black Feminist Criticism: Perspectives on Black Women Writers*. New York: Pergamon, 1985.

Clark, VeVe A. "Developing Diaspora Literacy and *Marasa* Consciousness." *Comparative American Identities: Race, Sex and Nationality in the Modern Text*. Ed. Hortense J. Spillers. New York: Routledge, 1991. 40–61.

Clifford, James, and George E. Marcus, eds. *Writing Culture: The Poetics and Politics of Ethnography*. Berkeley: U of California P, 1986.

Cobb, Martha. *Harlem, Haiti and Havana*. Washington: Three Continents, 1979.

Collins, Patricia Hill. *Black Feminist Thought: Knowledge, Consciousness, and the Politics of Empowerment*. New York: Routledge, 1990.

Conwill, Giles. "The Word Becomes Black Flesh: A Theoretical and Practical Paradigm for the Evangelization of Black Catholic Americans Based on Victor Turner's Concepts and Models of Dominant Symbol, Liminality, Communitas and Root Metaphor." Diss. Emory University, 1986

Cooper, Anna Julia. *A Voice from the South.* New York: Oxford UP, 1988.

Creel, Margaret Washingon. *"A Peculiar People:" Slave Religion and Community—Culture among the Gullahs.* New York: New York UP, 1988.

Dash, Julie. *The Making of an African American Woman's Film: Daughters of the Dust.* New York: The New P, 1992.

Davis, Arthur P., Joyce Ann Joyce, and J. Saunders Redding, eds. Vol. 2 *The New Cavalcade.* Washington, D.C. Howard UP, 1992.

Davis, Thadious M. *Nella Larsen: Novelist of the Harlem Renaissance.* Baton Rouge: Louisiana State UP, 1994.

Deren, Maya. *Divine Horsemen: The Living Gods of Haiti.* New York: McPherson, 1953.

Drake, St. Clair. *Black Folk Here and There: An Essay in History and Anthropology.* 2 vols. Berkeley: U of California P, 1987.

Drewal, Maragaret T., and Henry J. Drewal. "Composing Time and Space in Yoruba Art." *Word and Image: A Journal of Verbal/Visual Enquiry* 3 (1987): 225.

————. *Gelede: Art and Female Power among the Yoruba Women:* Bloomington: Indiana UP, 1983.

DuBois, W. E. B. *The Souls of Black Folk. The Oxford Reader: W. E. B. DuBois.* Ed. Eric J. Sundquist. Oxford UP, 1996.

————. *Darkwater. The Oxford Reader: W. E. B. DuBois.* Ed. Eric J. Sundquist. Oxford UP, 1996.

Eagleton, Terry. *Literary Theory: An Introduction.* Minneapolis: U of Minnesota P, 1983.

Fischer, Michael M. J. "Ethnicity and the Post-Modern Arts of Memory." *Writing Culture: The Poetics and Politics of Ethnography.* Ed. James Clifford and George A. Marcus. Berkeley: U of California P, 1986. 194–233.

Franklin, V. P. *Living Our Stories, Telling Our Truths.* New York. Oxford UP, 1995.

Frazer, James G. *The Golden Bough: A Study in Magic and Religion.* Vol. l. New York: Macmillan, 1911.

Freire, Paulo. *Pedagogy of the Oppressed.* New York: Herder, 1970.

Geertz, Clifford. *The Interpretation of Cultures.* New York: Basic Books, 1973.

Gilkes, Cheryl Townsend. "Mother to the Motherless, Father to the Fatherless:" Power, Gender, and Community in an Afrocentric Biblical Tradition. *Semeia* 47 (1989): 57–85.

Gordon, Deborah. "The Politics of Ethnographic Authority: Race and Writing in the Ethnography of Margaret Mead and Zora Neale Hurston." *Modernist Anthropology: From Fieldwork to Text.* Ed. Marc Manganaro. Princeton: Princeton UP, 1990.

Griaule, Marcel. *Conversations with Ogotemmeli: An Introduction to Dogon Religious Ideas.* London: Oxford UP, 1970.

Hemenway, Robert. *Zora Neale Hurston: A Literary Biography.* Urbana: U of Illinois P, 1977.

Head, Bessie. *A Woman Alone: Autobiographical Writings.* Portsmouth: Heinemann, 1990.

Herskovitz, Melville. *The Myth of the Negro Past.* Boston: Beacon, 1958.

———. *Dahomey.* New York, 1938.

Holloway, Karla F. C. *The Character of the Word: The Texts of Zora Neale Hurston.* Westport: Greenwood, 1987.

———. *Moorings & Metaphors: Figures of Culture and Gender in Black Women's Literature.* New Brunswick: Rutgers UP, 1992.

———. *Codes of Conduct: Race, Ethics, and the Color of Our Character.* New Brunswick: Rutgers UP, 1995.

hooks, bell. *Yearning: Race, Gender and Cultural Politics.* Boston: South End, 1990.

———. *Black Looks: Race and Representation.* Boston: South End, 1992.

———. *Killing Rage: Ending Racism.* New York: Henry Holt, 1995.

Hurston, Zora Neale. *Jonah's Gourd Vine.* 1934. New York: Lippincott, 1971.

——. *Mules & Men.* 1935. Bloomington: Indiana UP, 1978.

——. *Their Eyes Were Watching God.* Philadelphia: Lippincott, 1937.

——. *Tell My Horse.* Philadelphia: Lippincott, 1938.

——. *Moses Man of the Mountain.* 1939. Urbana: U of Illinois P, 1984.

——. *Dust Tracks on a Road.* 1942. Philadelphia: Lippincott, 1971.

——. *Seraph on the Suwanee.* New York: Scribner's, 1948.

——. *The Sanctified Church.* Berkeley: Turtle Island, 1981.

——. "The Eatonville Anthology." *Messenger,* 8 (Sept., Oct., Nov., 1926), 261–62, 197, 319, 332.

——. "Color Struck: A Play." *Fire!!* 1. (Nov., 1926), 7–15.

——. "How It Feels to Be Colored Me." *World Tomorrow,* 11 (May, 1928), 215–16.

——. "Race Cannot Become Great Until It Recognizes Its Talent." *Washington Tribune,* 1934: Dec. 29.

——. "The 'Pet Negro' System." *American Mercury,* 56 (May, 1943), 593–600.

——. "Negroes without Self-Pity." *American Mercury,* 57 (Nov., 1943), 601–3.

——. "My Most Humiliating Jim Crow Experience." *Negro Digest,* 2 (June, 1944), 25–26.

——. "Crazy for This Democracy." *Negro Digest,* 4 (Dec., 1945), 45–48.

——. "What White Publishers Won't Print." *Negro Digest,* 8 (Apr., 1950), 85–89.

Hutcheon, Linda. *The Politics of Postmodernism.* New York: Routledge, 1989.

Irele, Abiola. "In Praise of Alienation." In *The Surreptitious Speech: Presence Africaine and the Politics of Otherness, 1947–1987.* Ed. V.Y. Mudimbe. Chicago: U of Chicago P, 1992.

Jameson, Fredric. "Postmodernism and Consumer Society." Ed. Hal Foster. *The Anti-Aesthetic Essays on Postmodern Culture*. Port Townsend, Washington: Bay P, 1983.

Johnson, Barbara. "Thresholds of Difference: Structures of Address in Zora Neale Hurston." Baltimore: Johns Hopkins UP, 1987

Karanja, Ayana. "Zora Neale Hurston and Alice Walker: A Transcendent Relationship"—*Jonah's Gourd Vine* and *The Color Purple*. *Alice Walker and Zora Neale Hurston: The Common Bond*. Ed. Lillie P. Howard. Westport: Greenwood, 1993.

Lattin, Patricia Hopkins. "Naylor's Engaged and Empowered Narratee." In *CLA* Journal XLI (1998): 452–469.

Levine, Lawrence W. *Black Culture and Black Consciousness: Afro-American Folk Thought from Slavery to Freedom*. New York: Oxford UP, 1977.

Lionnet, Francoise. "Autoethnography: The An-archic Style of *Dust Tracks on a Road*." Ed. Dominick Lacapra. In *The Bounds of Race: Perspectives on Hegemony and Resistance*. Ithaca: Cornell UP, 1991.

―――. *Autobiographical Voices: Race, Gender, Self-Portraiture*. Ithaca: Cornell UP, 1989.

Locke, Alain, ed. *The New Negro: An Interpretation*. New York: Boni, 1925.

Lodge, David. *The Art of Fiction*. New York: Penguin, 1992.

Loriggio, Francesco. "Anthropology, Literary Theory, and the Traditions of Modernism." *Modernist Anthropology: From Fieldwork to Text*. Ed. Marc Manganaro. Princeton: Princeton UP, 1990. 215–242.

Lowe, John. *Jump at the Sun: Zora Neale Hurston's Cosmic Comedy*. Urbana: U of Illinois P, 1994.

MacGaffey, Wyatt. "Complexity, Astonishment and Power: The Visual Vocabulary of Kongo Minkisi." *Journal of Southern African Studies* 14:2 (January 1988): 188–203.

Marcus, George E. "Contemporary Problems of Ethnography in the Modern World System." *Writing Culture: The Poetics and Poli-*

tics of Ethnography. Ed. James Clifford and George E. Marcus. Berkeley: U of California P, 1986. 165.

McCall, John C. "Making Peace in Agwu." *Anthropology and Humanism* 18.2 (1993): 56–66.

Morrison, Toni. *Playing in the Dark: Whiteness and the Literary Imagination.* Cambridge: Harvard UP, 1992.

————. *Beloved.* New York: Knopf, 1987.

Mudimbe-Boyi, Elisabeth. "Harlem Renaissance and Africa: An Ambiguous Adventure." Ed. V. Y. Mudimbe. In *The Surreptitious Speech: Presence Africaine and the Politics of Otherness 1947–1987.* Chicago: U of Chicago P, 1992. 174–184.

Nahum D. Chandler. "The Figure of the X: An Elaboration of the DuBoisian Autobiographical Example." *Displacement, Diaspora, and Geographies of Identity.* Ed. Smadar Lavie & Ted Swendenburg. Durham: Duke UP, 1996.

Naylor, Gloria. *Mama Day.* New York: Ticknor and Fields, 1988.

Nichols, Charles H., ed. *Arna Bontemps, Langston Hughes: Letters 1925–1967.* New York: Dodd, Mead, 1980.

Out of the Forest. (The Kayapo) Dir. Terance Turner. "Disappearing World Series." PBS. 52 min. 1991.

Ogundipe-Leslie, Molara. *Re-creating Ourselves: African Women and Critical Transformations.* Trenton, N.J.: Africa World Press, 1994.

Ong, Walter. *Orality and Literacy: The Technologizing of the Word.* New York: Methuen, 1982.

Oyewumi, Oyeronke. *The Invention of Women: Making an African Sense of Western Gender Discourses.* Minneapolis: U of Minnesota P, 1997.

Parsons, Elsie Clews. *Spirit Cult in Hayti.* Paris, 1928.

Painter, Nell Irvin. *Sojourner Truth, a Life, a Symbol.* New York: Norton, 1994.

Pelton, Robert D. *The Trickster in West Africa: A Study of Mythic Irony and Sacred Delight.* Berkeley: U of California P, 1980.

Rabinow, Paul. "Representations are Social Facts: Modernity and Post-Modernity in Anthropology" in *Writing Ethnography: The Poetics and Politics of Ethnography.* Ed. James Clifford and George E. Marcus. U of California P, 1986. 234.

Rose, Dan. "Ethnography as a Form of Life: The Written Word and the Work of the World" in *Anthropology and Literature,* ed. Paul Benson. Urbana: U of Illinois P, 1993. 192–224.

Said, Edward W. *Culture and Imperialism.* New York: Knopf, 1993.

Seremetakis, C. Nadia, ed. *The Senses Still: Perception and Memory as Material Culture in Modernity.* Chicago: U of Chicago P, 1994.

Smith, Theophus H. *Conjuring Culture: Biblical Formations of Black America.* New York: Oxford UP, 1994.

Smitherman, Geneva. *Talkin' and Testifyin': The Language of Black America.* Boston: Houghton Mifflin, 1977.

Steady, Filomina Chioma, ed. *The Black Woman Cross-Culturally.* Cambridge: Schenkman, 1981.

Stepto, Robert B. *From behind the Veil: A Study of Afro-American Narrative.* Urbana: U of Illinois P, 1979.

Stetson, Erlene, ed. *Black Sister: Poetry by Black American Women, 1746–1980.* Bloomington: Indiana UP, 1981.

Stewart, John O. *Drinkers, Drummers, and Decent Folk: Ethnographic Narratives of Village Trinidad.* Albany: State U of New York P, 1989.

Sudarkasa, Niara. *The Strength of Our Mothers.* Trenton, N.J.: African World P, 1996.

Tate, Claudia. "Allegories of Black Female Desire; or, Reading Nineteenth-Century Sentimental Narratives of Black Female Authority." Ed. Cheryl Wall. *Changing Our Own Words: Essays on Criticism, Theory, and Writing by Black Women.* New Brunswick: Rutgers UP, 1989. 98–126.

Thiong'o, Ngugi Wa. *Decolonising the Mind: The Politics of Language in African Literature.* London: James Currey, 1986.

Thompson, Robert Farris, and Joseph Cornet. *The Four Moments of the Sun: Kongo Art in Two Worlds.* Vintage, 1984.

———. *Black Gods and Kings.* Bloomington: Indiana UP, 1976.

Todorov, Tzvetan. *Mikhail Bakhtin: The Dialogical Principle.* Trans. Wlad Godzich. Minneapolis: U of Minnesota P, 1984.

Trinh, Minh-ha T. *Woman, Native Other.* Bloomington: Indiana UP, 1989.

Turner, Edith. "Experience and Poetics in Anthropological Writing." Ed. Paul Benson. Urbana: U of Illinois P, 1993.

Turner, Victor. *Dramas, Fields, and Metaphors: Symbolic Action in Human Society.* Ithaca, N.Y.: Cornell UP, 1974.

Tyler, Stephen A. "Post-Modern Ethnography: From Document of the Occult to Occult Document." In *Writing Culture: The Poetics and Politics of Ethnography.* Ed. James Clifford and George E. Marcus. Berkeley: U of California P, 1986. 122.

Van Gennep, Arnold. *The Rites of Passage.* Chicago: U of Chicago P, 1960.

Walker, Alice. *The Color Purple.* San Deigo: Harcourt, Brace, Jovanich, 1982.

Walker, Sheila S. *Ceremonial Spirit in Africa and Afro-American Forms, Meanings and Functional Significance for Individuals and Social Groups.* Leiden: E. Brill, 1972.

Wall, Cheryl A., Comp. *Hurston: Folklore, Memoirs, & Other Writings.* New York: The Library of America, 1995.

———. *Hurston: Novels & Stories.* New York: The Library of America, 1995.

Waugh, Patricia. *Metafiction: The Theory and Practice of Self-Conscious Fiction.* New York: Routledge, 1993.

Weems, Clenora Hudson. *Africana Womanism: Reclaiming Ourselves.* Troy: Bedford P, 1993.

Weiner, Annette B. "Culture and Our Discontents." *American Anthropologist* 97.1 (1995): 14–20.

Wolf, Margery. *A Thrice Told Tale: Feminism, Postmodernism & Ethnographic Responsibility.* Stanford: Stanford UP, 1992.